The Canadian Issues Series

James Lorimer & Company has developed this series of original paperbacks to offer informed, up-to-date, critical introductions to key issues facing Canada and Canadians. Books are written specifically for the series by authors commissioned by the publisher on the basis of their expertise in a subject area and their ability to write for a general audience.

The 4'' × 7'' paperback format and cover design for the series offer attractive books at the lowest possible price. Special library hard-bound editions are also available. New titles are added to the series every spring and fall: watch for them in your local bookstore.

University and community college lecturers interested in forthcoming titles in the series should contact the Lorimer promotion manager.

Already in print:
(See page 235 for more details)

JOHN SEWELL

Police

Urban Policing in Canada

James Lorimer & Company, Publishers
Toronto 1985

ISBN 0-88862-743-2 paper
     0-88862-744-0 cloth

Cover design: Brant Cowie
Cover photo: The Stock Market

Canadian Cataloguing in Publication Data
  Sewell, John, 1940
     Police

  (Canadian Issues Series)

  Bibliography: p. 232

  1. Police - Canada.   2. Police power - Canada.   3.
  Criminal justice, Administration of - Canada.   I.
  Title.   II. Series: Canadian issues series (Toronto,
  Ont.)

  HV8157.S49 1985   363.2'0971   C84-099665-9

James Lorimer & Company, Publishers
Egerton Ryerson Memorial Building
35 Britain Street
Toronto, Ontario M5A 1R7

Printed and bound in Canada
6 5 4 3   90

Contents

Acknowledgements

My thanks to Peter Russell for getting me into this project, Clifford Shearing for helping sort out issues and material, and Doug Sanderson, who kindly gave me the office and the typewriter to pursue the first draft of the manuscript. This book is dedicated to Charlotte, my best critic and friend.

Introduction

Why a book on the police?

In 1981 I was teaching at York University after having failed to be re-elected as mayor of Toronto. As a member of city council — both as alderman and mayor — I had been a constant critic of policing in such areas as accountability, budgeting and police violence. Now out of political life, I received suggestions that I write a book on police. Given the amount of research required, that didn't make much sense unless I was also teaching the subject. I mentioned the idea, almost as an aside, to Dean Ron Bordessa of Atkinson College, and in the twinkling of an eye I was scheduled to teach ''Policing in Canada'' during the winter term.

The summer of 1981 was spent almost continuously in research. I had never had the opportunity to look at the voluminous literature on police — the number of books to wade through is almost limitless, ranging from tales of police bravery to police deviance. What surprised me was, first, there was no generally helpful book about policing in Canada and, second, so few books tried to look at policing in a comprehensive fashion. Most were narrow in approach and presented the American or British perspective.

The lack of useful books on policing was disturbing. The police function is the most important of all governmental activities — the keeping of some kind of order, the pursuit of criminal elements, the protection of the weak and gullible from the strong and ruthless, and the upholding of freedoms, including the right of dissent. Police are charged with these responsibilities, tasks that, taken together, loom larger than any other in the public realm. Yet I found few books that defined police functions, limits and feelings. There are scores of volumes about how governments work and don't work, the nature of the public health-care system, housing policies and the delivery of social welfare services. But when it comes to helpful analysis and critical comment about the police — silence.

This book's purpose is to remedy that omission. I have attempted to discuss the major issues about policing in Canada, show the different sides to the various arguments, and point out directions that seem promising. It is an introductory book meant for the general student of policing, the individual who wants a start at understanding the most important of government functions. It does not contain original research, and most of the thoughts are borrowed (with accreditation) from others. That is as it should be: many of the authors cited have spent much of their lives attempting to understand why police do the things they do, and why society looks on police in certain ways. I have tried to digest the work of those authors, and set down in simple language how they looked at police, society and crime.

In trying to provide a broad and general overview, I have been unable to deal with many specific issues.

The book does not touch on how homicide squads work, what drug squads do, how police work with informers, police communications systems, or forensic crime detection. Skipped over are the finer points of criminal law, espionage, the world of the secret service, the relation of police television shows to the public understanding of police, and other such matters. Police deviance is relegated a small place, one that is totally at variance with the vast amount of attention it receives in the media, but one that is more fitting to the role deviance plays in police activities.

I have attempted to focus on important issues that are rarely discussed in a comprehensive way: crime figures and what they mean; the relationship of police to crime; how police use discretion and what structure might be given to this wide range of personal decision making; different measures of police productivity and what can be expected of police; how the police are managed and the effects of that management on police morale; the "police personality" and the job society demands of police; the unasked questions of what society really wants police to do. If these questions were asked of any other branch of government service, the answers would be relatively easy to come by. Not so in policing, where questions like these receive skimpy attention.

Unfortunately, debate about policing matters is usually reduced to whether you're for the police or against them, as though being critical is by definition destructive. Politicians and public figures shy away from commenting on police matters because of the expected backlash. Policing authorities (like any branch of the civil service) have discouraged discussion about what they do, and they have been unusually successful in this. Public discussion about policing only takes place when some monstrous mistake is discovered or when an officer has performed a deed of great bravery or skill. They are talked about as either heroes or bums, and not much in between. I have specifically tried to avoid that kind of polarity here. The subject is just too important to view simplistically.

The lack of debate about policing is in large part a function of policing's importance. Much rests emotionally on policing in Canada — our national symbol is the RCMP — so that just like sex and religion, it's a subject polite conversation avoids. I hope that this book charts a new beginning in that regard. What *Police* lacks because of its brevity and its secondary nature, I hope it makes up in provoking a livelier discussion of its subject.

The book begins with a brief history of policing, in England and then in Canada. This chapter attempts to highlight many of the present problems in policing by showing how they were dealt with in the past.

Chapter 2 looks at crime statistics, what they mean, and how they relate to police work. The discussion deals with how crime is defined, theories about why some people become criminals while others don't, ideas about crime and the nature of society, the "dark figure" of crime, the criminal justice system, deterrence, and organized crime.

Chapter 3 explores the structure of a modern police department and analyzes what police officers and detectives actually do, with reference to recent studies on a Canadian police force. The specialization of police functions, recruitment, training and retraining, and police management systems are all surveyed. The chapter ends with a discussion of a growing phenomenon, the privately controlled police force.

Chapter 4 outlines various philosophies of policing

and grapples with the slippery question of police goals and objectives. Along the way we talk of productivity in police forces, how police use their powers and their discretion, and who ultimately runs police forces.

Police politics and personality are discussed in chapter 5, along with the ever-popular subjects of deviance and dirty tricks. An attempt is made to set these subjects in an appropriate context and to relate them to a general theory of police political action.

The last chapter suggests what kinds of reform are most needed in policing and how they might be achieved. This is the one prescriptive chapter. It is meant to be provocative — but at the same time reasonable. I believe that the nature of reforms required are not difficult to comprehend (although they might be difficult to implement) and would be supported by many rank-and-file officers. But these reforms require public attention if they are to become a reality.

1
The Development of Policing

In 1829 Sir Robert Peel introduced legislation in the English Parliament to establish a police force in the City of London. The legislation was a radical break from the past and created a new method of responding to the public desire for peace and order.

Since Anglo Saxon times, policing in Great Britain had evolved organically from the nature of social arrangements. While society changed, policing institutions showed more reluctance and lagged behind. By the eighteenth century, the organization of policing bore no relationship to the needs of the new society (although the nature of what policing should *be* was not entirely clear). In the first important step in almost six hundred years, Peel expected to set out a new model that would secure peace and order.

Yet this legislation was based on concepts outmoded even in 1829. Peel outlined certain principles, but they were as muddled and unclear as the ill-defined goals and objectives of a police force in the late decades of the twentieth century. Peel suggested the following principles for the new police force:

1. To prevent crime and disorder, as an alternative to their repression by military force and by severity of legal punishment.
2. To recognize always that the power of the police to fulfil their functions and duties is dependent on

public approval of their existence, actions and behaviour, and on their ability to secure and maintain public respect.

3. To recognize always that to secure and maintain the respect and approval of the public means also the securing of the willing co-operation of the public in the task of securing observance of laws.

4. To recognize always that the extent to which the co-operation of the public can be secured diminishes, proportionately, the necessity of the use of physical force and compulsion for achieving police objectives.

5. To seek and to preserve public favour, not by pandering to public opinion, but by constantly demonstrating absolutely impartial service to law, in complete independence of policy and without regard to the justice or injustices of the substance of individual laws; by ready offering of individual service and friendship to all members of the public without regard to their wealth or social standing; by ready exercise of courtesy and friendly good humour; and by ready offering of sacrifice in protecting and preserving life.

6. To use physical force only when the exercise of persuasion, advice and warning is found to be insufficient to obtain public co-operation to an extent necessary to secure observance of law or to restore order; and to use only the minimum degree of physical force which is necessary on any particular occasion for achieving a police objective.

7. To maintain at all times a relationship with the public that gives reality to the historic tradition that the police are the public and that the public are the police; the police being only members of the public who are paid to give full-time attention to duties which are incumbent on every citizen, in the interests of community welfare and existence.

8. To recognize always the need for strict adherence to police executive functions, and to refrain from even seeming to usurp the powers of the judiciary or aveng-

ing individuals or the state, and of authoritatively judging guilt and punishing the guilty.

9. To recognize always that the test of police efficiency is the absence of crime and disorder, and not the visible evidence of police action in dealing with them.

Many of these principles concern police behaviour that will obtain the approbation of the public. What was left unclear then, as it is now, is what — apart from seeking public favour—the real function of the police is to be in society. At the same time, the principles embody notions of policing that developed from Anglo Saxon times, ideas that continue to be expressed as society struggles to define police goals.

The Genesis of Policing

Peel referred to the "historic tradition that the police are the public and the public are the police." This tradition had evolved more than a thousand years earlier. In Saxon England (roughly the eighth to the eleventh century) there was a quasi contract between the king and his subjects. In return for allegiance, the king guaranteed the King's Peace. Best developed by King Edgar during his rule from 959 to 975, the King's Peace did not entail policing in the modern sense — it was assumed that somehow people would look after their own affairs — but aimed to create a stable society. The ruler did not want to be overthrown and sought fealty and allegiance. The people feared invasion and so gave allegiance to the king. Hence the bond, or social contract.

King Alfred made the idea of the King's Peace into something that more resembled internal protection, a system of mutual surety. An idea of community policing evolved, where the police were the public and the public the police. Alfred looked to the thane (land-owner) to produce a culprit thought to have committed a crime, and he also expected the thane to satisfy civil claims. In turn, for surety the thane counted on the freemen working his land. For their own protection from arbitrary decisions by the thane, freemen formed a tything, in which ten families stood as surety for one another. The tything agreed to produce one of its own if accused of a crime — or pay a fine. The tything was a social contract for surety and protection. Its members policed each other much as in today's Neighbourhood Watch programs, although the social bonds forged in this modern contract are much weaker.

The head of the tything was a tythingman, and a gathering of 100 tythingmen, no more surprisingly, formed a "hundred." The hundred met annually and elected a reeve who organized a court where complaints could be aired and disputes settled. The reeve from a shire or large landholding was known as the shire reeve, or sheriff. One notes the close relationship between a rudimentary system of justice and local government.

So began the Western notion of courts and law enforcement. The arrangements relied on a stable social order where families knew each other and could rely on one another for mutual protection. Punishments meted out for crimes were fierce, often involving muti-lation and death. The purpose was to deter imitators as well as to mark a person as a wrongdoer for all to see. There was a basic rough-and-easy democracy to the system, since the court system was in the control of the people through the hundred and tythings.

When the Normans invaded England in 1066 they immediately adapted the Saxon system to their agenda, which was to extend their authority throughout the conquered society. To ensure that every possible troublemaker was accounted for, the Normans required all men in tythings to register. Sheriffs were now appointed by, and accountable to, the Normans. The hundred court (renamed the Court of the Tourn) met annually. As well as continuing to deal with petty offences, it began to hear "presentments." The presentment was the report made by each tythingman of any suspect activity of interest to the sheriff or his Norman superiors, particularly seditious activity. The presentment was made to a group of twelve chosen from the hundred. This arrangement is continued in the modern notion of a grand jury, which hears preliminary evidence regarding a charge. Today the presentment exists in name and concept, but now relates to charges under the Criminal Code rather than the Normans' program of social control.

As a further control, each person was annually required to pledge allegiance to the Normans before the Court of the Tourn. Taken as one piece, the Norman adaptation of the Saxon social institutions was an effective form of social control. The sheriff levied heavy fines to show his superiors how jealous and tough he was (and to fill his own purse). Within a hundred years of the invasion, the Normans and Saxons had intermingled to the point where repressiveness eased. Some feudal lords were permitted to have their own courts, operating under an official who was appointed by the lord of the manor. Because these new "Court Leet" attempted to resolve local nuisances and social problems, they were extremely popular. One official of the Court Leet was the "comes stable," literally "master of the house," now vulgarized to "constable." His job was to make the presentment, and he was recognized by the crown as responsible for keeping the peace within the jurisdiction of the Court Leet. It appears that the constable was appointed by the crown, but responsible to more local interests.

The Court Leet did not exist everywhere. Many locales preserved the Court of the Tourn, with active sheriffs. A tension between the two approaches to law enforcement — one locally based and responsible to those most directly affected, the other installed by the king and often repressive — emerged. The same kind of tension is seen today in the question of whether city hall or provincial governments should have the final say in the running of the police force.

In England, that tension was resolved in 1215 when King John was forced by nobles to sign the Magna Carta. In that document the king agreed that fines levied by a sheriff had to bear some relationship to the severity of the crime committed. He further promised: "We will not make men judiciaries, constables, sheriffs or bailiffs, unless they understand the law of the land and are well disposed to observe it." The police and the justice system were beginning to take more formal shape.

The major changes embodied in the Magna Carta were built upon by the Statute of Westminster, enacted in 1285 under King Edward I. This statute is perhaps the most significant legislation in English history dealing with policing. It dictated the structure of policing until Peel's legislation of 1829. Four aspects of the statute were particularly important:

- The responsibility for prosecuting offences fell on the hundred and the Hundred Court in regard to all matters occurring within the physical boundaries of the hundred.

- The idea of the "watch" was established, setting in place a system that could, in reaction to the closing of the monasteries and the increased mobility of English society, arrest strangers and suspicious individuals. The watch was to keep a lookout for suspicious persons, much as police on patrol now do, save for the fact that members of the community were appointed in turn to serve on the watch as a shared social obligation. The act stated that if the watch "find cause of suspicion, they shall forthwith deliver him to the sheriff" and if there is no cause of suspicion then "he shall go quit." The latter phrase is a predecessor of the acquittal, when a suspect is set free.
- The constable was responsible for organizing the watch. He managed the watchmen and arranged to bring offenders before the sheriff and the courts. The constable tracked down offenders and saw to their security prior to trial. He also served court warrants. Like the watch, this position was filled by members of the community as required.
- The constable was responsible for "raising the hue and cry." If the constable was looking for an offender or stranger, the hue and cry obliged every man to join in the search. Every male was required to have an "assize of arms" (a weapon of some sort) to help in the hue and cry.

The statute also required that an area of 200 feet on either side of roads be cleared. Roads were recognized as a place where peace had to be secured, and thus the underbrush — a hiding place for robbers and highwaymen — was removed. Further, twenty-four wards were created in the City of London with six watchmen each, supervised by aldermen. The police and the local government were again developing common institutions.

The Statute of Westminster formalized the idea that a community could not police itself on an ad hoc basis, but that some kind of structure had to be established to order human affairs. No longer was it simply a matter of communities producing suspects when required. Because society was becoming more mobile, citizens were obliged, as a matter of public duty, to serve on a committee that monitored the behaviour and conduct of strangers coming into a neighbourhood. People were undertaking the police function, a function that was developing in response to changing social needs.

The statute makes no reference to the position of justice of the peace, an oversight historians have some difficulty explaining. The position had arisen in 1195 when King Richard I appointed knights who were to take an oath from each male to maintain the peace. As appointees of the crown, these knights carried considerable authority as they travelled about the country taking oaths. Quite quickly they began to exercise judicial powers, making decisions and meting out rough justice. They became known as justices of the peace. By 1360 there was a justice of the peace in every county. The justice prevented crime, made arrests, and heard and determined cases. Slowly over time the constable found he was responsible not to the sheriff but to this more noble figure, the justice of the peace.

Over the next several hundred years, cities swelled in size and work became more specialized. Society was more mobile, and the appearance of "strangers" — people not familiar to the community — became more and more frequent. The idea of the hue and cry became anachronistic, as craftsmen like weavers and blacksmiths found it difficult to leave their work to join a search for a stranger.

Further, the idea of rotating constables' duties among members of the community grew subject to abuse. The idea of a closed society, where there were recognized social obligations, was vanishing. More wealthy members of society hired stand-ins to serve their turn as constable. The constable's position deteriorated as the quality of stand-ins fell. By the end of the sixteenth century, the job was considered fit only for the unemployed, idiots and ne'er-do-wells. As the position became disreputable, constables became corrupt, using their powers for personal gain. Justices of the peace became more distanced from the crown, and they too were corrupted. The justice system atrophied as society and its economic system changed radically. Constables were not trusted; they were despised. Justices of the peace traded in justice, taking money for the laying and dismissal of charges. Since justices were paid by the case, it was in their interest to create as many cases — rightfully or wrongfully — as they could.

The Need for Reform

Not until the eighteenth century did the situation deteriorate enough to make reform a pressing necessity. Reform began with Henry Fielding, author of *Tom Jones* and other outstanding novels, who was appointed chief magistrate of Bow Street in London. Fielding both popularized reform and implemented it. He argued that magistrates should be paid by salary rather than by case, and was his own best example. He started a newspaper that recounted the crimes that he and his staff had solved or were trying to solve, and published a description of wanted suspects.

Perhaps of most significance is that Fielding secured funds to hire people to catch criminals. "The Bow Street runners" were concerned strictly with the apprehension of suspects; crime prevention was not part of the job. This was the first systematic attempt to arrest wrongdoers since the mutual-protection society of the Saxons. Fielding pointed to new directions in criminal law enforcement for a growing urban population where common bonds among communities had been broken and new kinds of social glue had not yet set. After Henry Fielding's death, reform continued under the influence of his blind brother, John.

The Gordon Riots in London in 1780 made it clear for all to see that society needed some institution that could be relied on to control unruly people and mobs and protect citizens from criminal attacks. In 1785 William Pitt introduced a bill in Parliament to establish a police force for London. The new organization would be charged with preventing crime and apprehending wrongdoers. The bill was greeted with a barrage of criticism that charged the new force would be a secret organization comparable to French gendarmes, with spies and informers trying to prop up a totalitarian state. The bill was withdrawn. (Similar complaints are made today by many who feel that police are indeed a political force, acting on behalf of those in power rather than pursuing independent justice.)

The death of Pitt's bill did not halt reform. The Bow Street runners expanded to include mounted patrols outside London that searched out highwaymen — an early example of preventative policing. This proved so successful that "unmounted horse patrols" were established in London itself. These patrols were on foot (as the name so directly suggests), operating only at night until 1820, when daylight patrols were added.

These were carried out by men who were one step removed from being highwaymen themselves; the justice they meted out was rough. And their numbers were small. While London's population at the turn of the century was 1.5 million, the force boasted no more than 450 men.

The impetus for the next advance in policing came from the booming shipping business on the Thames River. Companies looking for ways to protect their property and goods established a private marine force. The force was so effective that it was put under public control in 1800: thus successful policing began in the private sector and then moved to the public. (Ironically, today policing is moving in the opposite direction, as "security firms" take over more and more of policing's patrol functions. This trend is discussed in chapter 3.)

The clamour for some kind of publicly controlled policing organization became louder. As the Industrial Revolution gathered steam and produced wealth, its beneficiaries — a burgeoning middle class — complained about the difficulty of walking safely on streets populated by thieves, beggars, prostitutes and salesmen.

In the late eighteenth century the eminent British philosopher Jeremy Bentham had argued the utility of prevention over punishment. A police force should be used to stop crime before it happens, deterring criminals with the fear of discovery and apprehension. This was the rationale that many had waited for, an approach distinct from the French experience, where police officers served those who ruled rather than the law, and thus were considered a real political threat to the populace. Police magistrate and reformer Patrick Colquhoun argued for the separation of policing from the judicial function on the grounds that making one body responsible for apprehension, conviction *and* punishment hardly represented disinterested justice.

By 1829 England was ready for change. While Pitt's proposal of 1785 had been stoutly resisted, the legislation introduced by Peel to create the London police force was readily adopted. This bill did not accomplish the separation of the judiciary from the police: in fact, it required that the chief police officer be a justice of the peace. That severance came in England in 1839. In Canada the confusion Colquhoun complained of continues: some provinces require that one or more members of a police commission be a judge.

So began the modern era of policing. With minor variations, the policing model set out in Peel's legislation has continued to serve communities for more than 150 years.

Policing in Canada

English ideas about policing were brought holus-bolus across the Atlantic Ocean and put in place in North America. Thus, early American settlements used the constable for apprehension and the watch for minimal surveillance. As different communities developed their own character and local government took root, communities began to elect their own police chiefs. A very decentralized policing tradition became established. Today, many American cities continue to elect important figures in the judicial system, and the decentralization — some would say disorganization — of policing continues.

In Canada, the British colonialists employed night watchmen, and the function of keeping the peace was in the hands of the colonial army. Town and city coun

cils followed the English lead and, after Peel's legislation was adopted in 1829, established their own police
forces, usually headed up by the mayor and several
aldermen. Social disturbances in the 1840s and early
1850s led to the creation of police forces of a more
than local nature. For instance, the North West Mounted
Police were formed in 1873 to ensure an orderly development of the Canadian West.

The function of early police forces in Canada were
eclectic, to say the least. In 1892 Regina appointed its
first constable. His duties included acting as dog
catcher, licence inspector, health and sanitation
inspector, and volunteer fireman. Only ten years later,
when the town's population had swollen to 3,000, did
the force expand to four officers. Similar stories are
told in all Canadian cities.

As cities grew, policing became more important. In
the late 1850s the Upper Canada (later Ontario)
government required cities to establish police forces
— and at the same time took away from the municipalities the power to control their own police. Instead
Upper Canada established local Boards of Commissioners of Police, burdened with a majority of provincial appointees. That change has been a bone of
contention ever since, flaring into open debate at least
once a decade as municipalities have sought to control
this important function, which — it has turned out —
is largely funded through municipally raised property
taxes. There is some suggestion that the 1858 legislation was enacted to keep "politics" out of policing,
but it may simply be the result of the province moving
in to assume power over a function it saw as crucial
to its control of cities.[1]

Urban policing was seen as an adjunct of local
government, and as the latter grew, so did the former.

When a city was large and healthy, so was the police force. Thus, as Toronto's population enlarged to half a million at the end of the nineteenth century, the police force reached 890 officers by 1890 and 999 officers a decade later. When a city was small, just getting on its feet, the policing function shared the same characteristics, as the example of Regina cited above shows. Only as cities matured were their forces relieved of overseeing licensing and the like, leaving them with tasks related to criminal justice and the preservation of order.

The policing of the areas outside of cities and towns proved more difficult, particularly since policing had been conceived in the English-speaking world as very much an urban institution.[2] Upper Canada itself did not enter the field until 1859. A government detective was hired to augment the magistrates appointed to deal with the border problems arising from the American Civil War, and it was only in 1877 that the Constables Act was passed to permit constables to be appointed throughout the province. But even with a provincial population of two million by the 1890s, less than two dozen constables were active. Whatever crime was occurring could obviously be handled by the city police forces.

But all that began to change as new frontiers opened up in Ontario early in the twentieth century. In 1903 silver was discovered at Cobalt, and the prospectors rushing to Northern Ontario were followed by constables. By 1909 the Ontario Provincial Police (OPP) was established. Staffing was limited in the early days — even by 1929 it was less than three hundred — and expenses were covered by the fines levied. (In 1918 revenues exceeded costs by $21,004.)

It appears that the OPP had two main tasks in addition to criminal law enforcement. One was enforcing liquor laws, both those that allowed liquor under certain circumstances and those that didn't (after the Ontario Temperance Act was passed in 1916). A second was policing strikes, apparently on the side of management — the OPP kept workers in their place and blamed unrest on Communist infiltrators. An official history of the force contains a dismal litany of police interventions — against war veterans who couldn't find work in the early Twenties, transients in Northern Ontario, Stratford furniture workers, Cornwall textile workers, and even more recent action, such as against the strikers at Fleck Manufacturing in 1978.

During this time, technology radically altered the way policing was carried on in Ontario and in the rest of the country. Cars first saw service in 1920, then speedboats, and in 1927 airplanes. Radios were introduced in 1947 and the walkie-talkie three years later. By then, the OPP had grown to a force one-thousand strong. By the mid-1970s it was five times that size.

The development of policing in Canada as a whole roughly paralleled that in Ontario, with a distance of some years, although the dearth of useful literature on the subject makes it difficult to provide any kind of insightful history of what happened and why. Clearly, as railways were built and waves of immigrants moved across the country, the new pressures disrupted traditional social patterns. In Western Canada, the response was the establishment of the North West Mounted Police in 1873. The Canadian government had just purchased the Prairies from the Hudson's Bay Company, and British Columbia, which had been promised a trans-Canada railway, had just joined Confederation. The Mounted Police would help to establish a federal presence in land whose Native People were too often exploited by American traders. Indeed, as some have pointed out, "many people assume that the NWMP were founded in response to the Cypress Hills Massacre, when American whiskey traders murdered several Assiniboine Indians in May 1973."[3] In what has become a hallmark of Canadian culture, it is generally assumed that the police were sent to establish order so that liberty and freedom could then be enjoyed — in stark contrast to the American notion that freedom and liberty come first, with order following far behind. Given the lack of governmental institutions, the Mounted Police became the symbol of public intervention, of order in what might have been chaos.

Yet the picture is not quite that simple. As Lorne and Caroline Brown forcefully point out, the NWMP was seen as a force that would keep peace between the Indians and the settlers so that economic development would then proceed. The force played a considerable role in pacifying the Indians, and when the Métis rebellion led by Louis Riel occurred in 1885, the NWMP joined with the army to suppress it. There are several notable occasions when the force acted to break strikes against the Canadian Pacific Railway, a skill honed further against strikers during the Winnipeg General Strike of 1919 when the local police force — apparently keeping up a widespread tradition of local forces not intervening against local workers[4] — refused to make arrests and restore order. The NWMP was used to fire into a crowd of pro-strike veterans and break the strike.

By the end of the century, the North West Mounted Police had 750 officers. In 1920, when it had grown to more than 1,600, its name was changed to the Royal Canadian Mounted Police. It provided virtually all policing in Western Canada save for some of the growing settlements that opted for their own locally controlled force. The RCMP has also served as the country's secret service and has played a considerable role in controlling political dissent (see, for instance, chapter 4), as well as intervening on the side of management in labour disputes in virtually every province when called upon.

The RCMP continues to provide many policing services to Western Canada and to the Maritimes on a contract basis. It is responsible for policing all provinces except Ontario and Quebec on a provincial basis, and provides local policing for smaller municipalities as requested. In 1982 the federal government indicated that it would be gradually increasing the cost of this contract policing in order to recover 100 per cent of its costs (in 1981 it recovered 56 per cent). As municipalities and provinces are forced to pay more and more of the real costs of policing, they might decide to establish their own provincial and urban forces, as is now happening in Newfoundland.

Ontario and Quebec have their own provincial police forces. As noted above, the Ontario force began to take shape in the closing years of the nineteenth century and only blossomed during World War Two, when many municipalities asked the province to assume policing duties.[5] The Ontario Provincial Police was formally born in 1946, when legislation clarified the relation between local forces and provincial policing. The OPP was to oversee the operation of local forces by providing management advice, coordination and some degree of standardization, as well as assuming responsibility for much police training.

The Ontario Police Commission (OPC) was formed in 1961, in response to pressure from municipalities that wanted some governing force to be responsible for the OPP. At the same time, a coordinating body was needed to deal with what was seen as a rising tide of organized crime activity, and the OPC was to fill that role. Since then, the OPC has been the final court of appeal on disciplinary matters, and it has acted as a management consultant to many smaller local forces.

Provincial policing in Quebec has followed a path remarkably similar to that in Ontario, with a rudimentary force in place in the nineteenth century, but a formal organization not established until much later. The Quebec Provincial Police was established by legislation in 1968.

The number of police at the local, provincial and federal levels has grown rapidly in Canada. By 1980 there were more than 58,000 public police personnel in Canada, with a total expenditure of $1.7 billion.[6] Police organizations have grown with virtually no questions having been asked about their functions, and little demanded in the way of accountability. Public policy regarding policing matters is rarely debated, and the expansion of police services has not been subject to the same kinds of scrutiny as other governmental activities. As will be seen, it is difficult to determine when policing is performed well, given the paucity of research available and the limited discussion of police issues.

The modern police force has a relatively short tradition on which to rely. References to forms of social control extant in Saxon England — whether made by Peel or by today's commentators who cite Peel as though the situation in the 1820s were relevant to that in the 1980s — are not helpful in illuminating present questions and dilemmas about policing. Indeed, basic data about the police role in dealing with crime is not readily known, thus obscuring the real function of police work. It is to that subject — crime and police — that we now turn.

2
Crime and Police

The public attitude to police is largely shaped by the perception that crime is commonplace and getting worse every year. There is a fear of the ''dark figure of crime,'' a fear that often overshadows any desire to know what the real situation is. This chapter attempts to put crime — its statistics, causes, explanations and effects — in a perspective that will give a better handle on an understanding of police.

The Statistical Picture of Crime

Society has but a sketchy picture of crime and its effects. Contrary to common assumptions, the actual incidence of criminal activity — at least as recorded by police — is not of epidemic proportions. Although specific individuals may bear a heavy personal cost, overall the amount of harm and damage is quite limited. The following statements from the solicitor general of Canada in 1981 bear out these generalizations:[1]

- Victims are compensated (by insurance, for example) for approximately half of their losses from crime.
- In assault cases, only one in twelve victims is seriously enough harmed to require medical attention. Most assaults do not cause physical harm to victims.
- Approximately two-thirds of all break-and-enter

occurrences result in losses of less than $200, and of these, half involve no loss at all.

- For the majority of crimes, women and the elderly are less frequently victimized than men or younger persons, but they suffer more from the *fear* of crime.

Reading the daily press does not lead one to such conclusions, but they are borne out by the statistics. To provide easy comparison between countries and cities of varying size, crime measurements are usually made per 100,000 population. For instance, for every 100,000 people in Canada in 1979, there were 4,000 property offences — that is, break and enter, theft, and motor vehicle theft. While the increase in the previous ten years was substantial (from 2,750), the rate is remarkably low, given all of the shoplifting, bicycle thefts and comparable incidents that people in cities have grown used to.

Violent offences — murder, manslaughter, attempted murder, wounding, robbery, rape — have a rate of about 112 per 100,000. While this rate has almost doubled since 1969, it is thought that some of the increase may be due to better reporting by both victims and police authorities. The actual number of Criminal Code offences on Canada in 1979 was as follows:

Violent Offences	*147,528*
Murder	587
Manslaughter	39
Attempted murder	754
Rape	2,291
Other sexual offences	10,042
Wounding	2,295
Other assaults (not indecent)	110,616
Robbery	20,899

Property Offences	*1,186,697*
Break and enter	296,437
Theft, motor vehicle	91,445
Theft, over $200	169,950
Theft, under $200	516,184
Stolen goods	20,997
Frauds	91,684
Other Criminal Code Offences	*521,046*
Total Criminal Code Offences	*1,855,271*

One notes that more than two-thirds of violent offences were assaults, and as we've seen, less than 15,000 of those required medical treatment. Almost one-half of all property offences were thefts of less than $200. Once these activities are discounted, the amount of worrisome criminal activity adds up to very little — less than 60,000 serious violent offences a year in Canada.

Figures are analyzed slightly differently in the popular booklet *Crime in Ontario*.[2] Violent offences in 1979 accounted for 5.8 per cent of total crime, and that figure is broken down in the following way:

Robbery	0.50 per cent
Sexual offences	0.47 per cent
Homicide/attempted murder	0.04 per cent
Assaults (not indecent)	4.80 per cent

Assuming that most assaults are relatively trivial, serious violent crime accounts for less than 2 per cent of all crime. Judging by official statistics alone, serious criminal activity isn't what it's cracked up to be. (Though later in this chapter we will see that these statistics do not tell the whole story.)

Crime is not distributed evenly across the country. The rate of violent crime in British Columbia (925/100,000) is more than double that in Quebec (460/100,000) or the Atlantic provinces (480/100,000). This rise in rates from east to west is also reflected in property crime, with the low end in the Atlantic provinces (3,300/100,000) and the high in British Columbia (7,000/100,000). Ontario rates are lower than in the Prairies. One explanation of this variable rate is the "Go west" phenomenon. Individuals who have difficulty fitting into an existing social structure in North America have usually headed west, and significant numbers of those who have the most difficulty end up on the West Coast, where, due in part to this influx, the incidence of crime — and suicide — is highest.

Rates of property crime appear to be higher in towns and villages than they are in either smaller cities or larger cities, at least in Ontario.[3] The reverse holds true for violent crime, although only marginally so. What lies behind these comparisons is difficult to determine. They could simply reflect different methods of reporting incidences, or different police practices on the street. Or perhaps behaviour patterns differ depending on the size of the community.

Canadian crime rates are exceedingly low compared with those in the United States.[4] As noted above, the rate of violent crime in Canada in 1979 was 122/100,000. In the same year in the United States, it was 525/100,000, more than four times the Canadian rate. The murder rate in Canada is one-third of that in the U.S. and one-quarter of that in the southern states. Canadian rates of rape and robbery are less than one-third the American. Rates of break and enter and theft are comparable in the two countries. Needless to say, rates do vary from community to community.

A number of explanations can be offered for these differences, but by themselves none seem convincing. For instance, it is argued that in the United States, racial discrimination results in more stressful interpersonal relations, and thus more criminal activity. Guns are much more widely available in the U.S. than in Canada. In the free-enterprising U.S., people care more about money, and thus are drawn into crime. Americans live with a wider gulf between the haves and the have-nots, leading to crime undertaken out of sheer desperation.

Wider, more political explanations have been offered. In Canada the formative social principle is expressed as "peace, order and good government," a phrase redolent with social cohesion: the individual fits in rather than standing apart. In the United States the comparable phrase is "life, liberty and the pursuit of happiness," much more evocative of the freedom of the individual — and the deviant — to carry a gun and seek his or her own place in the social order. The American ethos can be seen as more accommodating to criminal, antisocial behaviour, since a lower value is placed on the well-being of society than on the freedom of the individual.

These points are not advanced here to give them credibility, but rather to indicate the range of explanations that are offered for the dramatic differences in crime statistics between two countries that share a very thin border. While none of these answers are entirely satisfying, better ones have yet to surface.

The effect of crime is much less devastating on people's lives than day-to-day accidents, of which those involving automobiles take the heaviest toll. The rate of 70 violent non-natural deaths per 100,000 in Canada is roughly broken down as follows:

Murder	2
Suicide	13
Traffic accidents	18
Other accidents	36

On the basis of these figures, it is possible to argue that to improve individual security and preserve life, society should devote more attention to reducing all the variables of violent non-natural deaths *other* than murder.

It is often stated that while the figures describing crime are not in themselves worrisome, the rate of increase in those figures is. Violent crime doubled in Canada between 1965 and 1979 (it tripled in the United States), and from 1969 to 1979, property offences climbed about 30 per cent. The Ontario government concludes that the rate of increase in offences is in the order of 4 per cent per annum. The reasons for the upward trend, and why year-to-year variations occur, are not fully understood. But it would be misleading to say that crime is zooming uncontrollably upward.

A note of caution should be added regarding crime figures. There are serious problems in the collection and interpretation of these statistics, arising from the following factors:

- Police do not lay charges in all cases, even though they might have a suspect they know can be convicted. For instance, they might forgo a lesser charge for something more serious. In such situations, the smaller crime obviously does not get included in the calculations.
- Many crimes, especially rape, some shoplifting and assault, are not reported to the police because victims might think that the act of reporting will cause more social dislocation than the crime itself.

- In many situations, police lay multiple charges in the hope that at least one charge will stick. In some cases, conviction results from a negotiated set of facts rather than from the real facts, whatever they might be.
- Differing administrations have different standards and priorities for data collection and interpretation. One body of thinking says that crime has not increased in the last decade, but that police have become much more efficient at collecting data and having victims report incidents. While it is impossible to judge this argument, if it is valid, crime might have actually decreased.
- Comparisons between different jurisdictions are difficult because of different laws and procedures. American jurisdictions define certain crimes (like aggravated assault) differently than in Canada, permitting only rough comparisons. Further, reporting arrangements run from poor to excellent, although in Canada, government officials are making a concerted effort to standardize the collection and reporting of crime statistics.

Crime by Sex, Age and Ethnicity

Whatever the inadequacies of crime reporting in Canada, it is clear that involvement in crime is a function of sex and age. Young males are much more likely than others to be on the receiving end of a criminal charge.

The number of females charged with criminal offences in Canada is substantially less than the number of males. Nationwide, in 1979, 25,000 females were charged with "serious" offences (involving physical harm or theft), while 115,000 males were charged. Of all crimes in developed countries, about 15 per cent are committed by females.[5]

When criminal acts are reviewed in categories, males have a strong lead in all areas except shoplifting and trying to pass bad cheques. Ontario data for 1979 show that 8,905 males were convicted of shoplifting, compared with 9,110 females; 4,162 males were convicted of writing bad cheques, compared with 5,008 females.

A number of theories have been developed to explain this phenomenon:[6]

- The nineteenth-century Italian criminologist Cesare Lombroso argued that women are more conservative than men, more wedded to a stable social structure, and therefore less attracted to deviant and chancy behaviour. He used as an analogy the male sperm, which moves around and is very active, and the female egg, which remains in one place and is passive. This kind of theory — depending as it does on the concept of women's natural subservience — is generally discredited today.
- The English criminologist Leon Radzinowicz — perhaps the most widely recognized expert in his field in the mid-twentieth century — argues that women have fewer opportunities for crime in the existing social structure. He cites the fact that when women were forced to take over most civilian activities in Germany during the Second World War, their crime rates came closer to those of males. This theory would argue that as women are permitted to participate more fully in society, they will also achieve equality in crime. While female crime has increased in the last decade, it remains well below 50 per cent of all criminal activity.

- A third theory is that women are biologically more submissive than men. Radzinowicz cites some experimental evidence indicating that women are more vulnerable than men to social censure and disapproval — hence they are less likely to risk criminal behaviour. While this explanation and the first one are mutually supportive, both seem wedded to the notion that women are naturally inferior to men, an explanation few can (or at least should) accept today.

- The converse explanation is that women are stronger than men and more responsible socially. This line of reasoning has been evoked frequently during the twentieth century in the name of stopping war (for example, if women were in charge, there would be no war) and other causes. Unfortunately, this argument suffers from the same weakness as those based on female passivity — they are rooted more in sexual politics than science.

These theories attempt to explain the difference on biological, social or moral grounds. None are particularly convincing, although the second has some attraction. One has to conclude that a number of these factors must be taken together to understand why women are so underrepresented in crime statistics.

Similar questions emerge in respect to youth. The young, particularly young males, are overrepresented in crime statistics. Again, a number of theories have been advanced by way of an explanation:

- A common suggestion is that the young are daring, full of uncritical enthusiasm, high energy and a lack of foresight. These characteristics lead them into criminal acts before they realize what they have done. Individual cases supporting this explanation are not hard to come by. Yet one might argue that if youths have no control over their actions, they should not be blamed for what they do. This explanation says nothing about the great number of young people who *don't* get involved in crime. How does one account for them?

- The nineteenth-century Belgian criminologist Adolphe Quetelet argued that criminal behaviour in the young is a result of impulsive actions that spring from the conflicts of adolescence. "The propensity to crime," he wrote, "must be at its maximum at the age when strength and passions have reached their height yet when reason has not acquired sufficient control to master their combined influence." In other words, youthful crime is the result of a natural disequilibrium — small solace to anyone trying to reduce such wrongdoing to a set of causal relationships.

- A third, commonly heard, explanation is that the young are too pampered, their lives are too easy, and crime makes up for the excitement that is lacking. This might explain why certain individuals turn to crime, just as poverty is often cited as a cause. Yet we are still without any general explanation of why young males are overrepresented.

- A related argument is that young people turn to crime because there are few satisfying work opportunities. Is this a version of the old rubric "The devil makes work for idle hands"? Perhaps yes — and it also resembles the argument that if immigrants are not permitted to participate in legitimate economic activity, they'll find an economic activity of their own, even if it is organized crime.

- Many argue that peer pressure drives youths to crime:

"He was in with the wrong crowd," one hears. Yet data indicate that youth crime rarely involves a group — it is most often carried off singly or in pairs.[7] A study of 10,000 youths in Philadelphia concluded that one-third came to the attention of the police, and of those, one-half kept out of trouble. Only 6 per cent of the total were recidivists. This relatively small group (of 627 youths) was responsible for half of all recorded crime in the group, including two-thirds of all violent crimes.

- A different approach relates the preponderance of youth crime to police behaviour: because police pick on youths, they are overrepresented in criminal statistics. It is frequently argued that police lay charges against youths when similar transgressions involving older people are overlooked or forgotten. (Perhaps females are underrepresented because police are lax with them.) In his study of Peel Regional Police, Richard Ericson gives some evidence supporting this proposition.[8]

This potpourri of explanations mixes common wisdom and academic thought. On their own, none seem capable of offering a comprehensive explanation: they do not account for the great bulk of youth who are *not* involved in crime. The reasons for succumbing to crime may be clear on an individual basis, but beyond that it seems difficult to move with certainty. One aspect of youthful crime that can be predicted confidently was pointed out by the American criminologist James Q. Wilson:

> By 1990 about half a million fewer eighteen-year-old males will be living in this country [the U.S.] than were living here in 1979. As everyone knows, young males commit proportionately more crimes than older

ones. Since it is the case in general that about 6 per cent of young males become chronic offenders; if each chronic offender commits ten offences (a conservative estimate) per year, we will have a third of a million fewer crimes from this age group alone.[9]

Certain "ethnic" minority groups are also over-represented in crime figures. This phenomenon may give us a clearer idea of why some groups are more involved in crime than others. In Canada Native Peoples constitute 0.5 per cent of the general population — and 6.5 per cent of the prison population.[10] Various studies in Canada and the United States reveal a similar discrepancy for other minorities. Part of the blame for this pattern can be laid at the door of institutionalized racism in society. At the same time, Natives' response to their place in an alien society aggravates their already dire situation. Heather Robertson describes this catalysis in her powerful book *Reservations Are for Indians*:

> Young Indian delinquents are described as being typical of their race and culture. They are not really delinquent: they are Indian. They share the values of their society, and they only get into trouble when they come into contact with the white man's law. Coming into contact with the police seems to be, from the growing number of Indians in jail and foster homes, an essential part of Indian culture.
>
> The conventional term for these antagonistic Indians is "sociopath." It describes violent anti-social behaviour which does not seem to be a product of mental illness, but of social environment. A sociopath, viewed in terms of the society to which he is antagonistic, is described as showing emotional insecurity, compulsive behaviour and a need for immediate gratification of impulses....This behaviour is totally pleasure-seeking. Passions are intense and

expressed in extreme physical ways — crime, destruction, fights, lies, cheating — and destructive acts repeated again and again.[11]

What's lacking from all the diagnoses of criminal activity that we've seen is a definition of the *nature* of crime. What behaviour is deemed criminal? Does it vary depending on time, place and person? These are the questions to which we now turn.

What Is Crime?

The criminal justice system attempts to deal with three kinds of problems:

- What conduct should be designated as criminal?
- What determination must be made before a person can be found to have committed a crime?
- What should be done with persons who are found to have committed criminal offences?

Our legislative bodies pass laws that provide partial answers to all three questions. Within the leeway provided by the law, judges and the court system make decisions about the kinds of proof, the evidence that will be admitted in making a decision, and the punishment.

The entry point to the criminal justice system is usually the police. Police are the first officials on the scene of a crime; they make the arrest, question the accused, gather evidence, and bring the accused to court. One critic — Jerome Skolnick — argues that the police are the key players in the criminal justice system. If the police consider a person to be guilty, then that person will be convicted of something considered appropriate by the police.[12]

Yet finding the answer to the first question — what conduct should be designated as criminal — is not easy. There have been radical shifts in how crime is defined and, accordingly, how society should deal with it. Radzinowicz defines five schools of thought on this question:[13]

The *liberal* approach emerged in the eighteenth century as a reaction to tradition and authority, where a crime was anything that the king defined as such. This approach — outlined by the Italian Cesare Beccaria and then adopted as the basis of the Code Napoleon in France in 1810 — relied on the idea of "natural rights" and "natural laws" that all thinking people would recognize as characterizing a civilized society. Individuals should be restricted as little as possible in deed and thought, providing their actions did not interfere with the rights of others. Individuals were treated as rational, knowing both what they were doing and the consequences of their actions. Since everyone was thought to know the difference between right and wrong, everyone knew when they were *doing* wrong. If one did wrong, it was only appropriate that punishment would follow to ensure that others were deterred from acting in a similar fashion. The liberal approach found widespread support in Europe and also in the United States, where it formed the basis of the 1865 Criminal Code.

Critics of the liberal approach emerged in Italy in the late nineteenth century, led by seminal thinkers like Cesare Lombroso, Enrico Ferri and Raffaelo Garofolo. They argued — just as Darwin had in the natural sciences — that people were affected by the society in which they lived, that it was not simply a matter of everyone knowing what was right and wrong. Choices are determined by time, place and acculturation, and people are not as free to choose between options as liberals would have them believe.

The reaction to the liberal approach was *positivism*, a school of thought named after the ideas of Auguste Comte. Positivism held that the best way to reduce crime was to reform society, rather than punish wrong-doers. Moral guilt as determined in the liberal camp didn't make much sense to the positivists, who looked more closely at social problems and their effect on behaviour.

The positivist modification of the liberal approach was not entirely satisfying. After all, as critics like the French sociologist Emil Durkheim argued, every society has crime. No culture has been perfected to the point of ridding itself of criminal behaviour. Perhaps crime is more natural than is commonly believed. A society without crime would be so authoritarian, so intolerable, as to be impossible. From this line of thought emerged the *sociological* view, based on the observation that every society houses criminal elements. The presence of crime indicates that a society has attained some degree of advancement, since the crime itself reflects that some differences of behaviour are admitted, although not all are condoned.

The sociological view of crime began to change perceptions about the nature of criminal punishment. Punishment should not be exacted because of the infringement of a moral law (as in the liberal view), but rather to reinforce collective values and particularly the collective idea of good. Crime exists as a foil for good actions.

The development of the *socialist* view of crime paralleled that of the sociological view in the late nine-teenth century. While it was inspired by Marx, the socialist perspective on crime was first formulated in

1916 by Dutch philosopher William Adrian Bonger. It holds that capitalism produces crime because it forces people to compete with each other. When capitalism is finally replaced with socialism, the socialists argue, crime will wither to almost nothing. Unfortunately, no state appears close to achieving genuine socialism, so it is difficult to judge if this theory actually holds. It is known that countries that consider themselves to be approaching the socialist ideal have rates of crime differing little from capitalist countries, but since in practice they stray so far from the ideal, they should not be used to disprove the socialist assumption.

A fifth theory of crime that emerged in the 1970s has been dubbed the *radical* approach. Thinkers like Ian Taylor, Paul Walton and Jock Young argue that crime is part of a wider field of human deviance, including mental illness, personality disorders and even stuttering. Deviant behaviour should be interpreted in light of what it means to deviants themselves: their criminal acts are not entirely unreasonable, given the pressures they are responding to. An example is the battered wife who kills her husband. Criminal acts are simply forms of behaviour that the state decides it wants to suppress, no matter what their cause. For the radicals, the best society is one where individuals can act with minimal restraint and be themselves.

The radical approach begins to complete the circle, almost returning to the perceptions that led to the liberal definition of crime and the idea of the natural man. These five theories define virtually all of the ground there is, and other ideas can find a place within this spectrum.

These theories are often invoked in a popular way to define and explain various acts. Many suggest that if there were less poverty, crime would decrease (the positivist view). Some blame the accused, saying he or she should have known better (the liberal approach). Others say that crimes of passion are more closely related to passion than to crime (a widely held view that fits well in the radical camp). In many cases, several of these approaches will be drawn on at the same time.

As helpful as these five ways of looking at criminal behaviour are, none provide a workable definition of crime. What is it, and why are certain acts defined as being criminal in nature? Finding easy answers to these questions is impossible, unless one settles for the most basic of definitions: crime is conduct forbidden by law and for which punishment is prescribed. Such a definition is obviously flawed, since it includes the full range of social transgressions, down to breaking municipal bylaws regarding housing standards and levels of maintenance. (Some bylaws even prohibit weeds above a specified height!) These are instances where conduct is forbidden and punishment prescribed, but hardly crime in common parlance.

Provincial laws define the rules of the road for drivers, the controls on alcohol, and the regulations about eggs, butter, animals and the environment. Violations of these laws fit the definition of crime, but are not normally considered as such by society. And social perceptions do change. More so today than fifteen years ago, people think that the dumping of dangerous chemicals in sewers and streams is criminal in nature.

There are a host of laws at the federal level: the Criminal Code, narcotics-control legislation, restrictions on the suppression of competition among companies, and on and on. Many of these laws are normally considered to proscribe criminal activity, while others less obviously deal with the ''criminals.'' What, for instance, is to be made of a federal law — enacted in the late 1970s — that prevents public discussion of the government's involvement in a worldwide uranium cartel? Is that a law defining criminal behaviour?

The range of law is very broad, and rules vary on determining when the law has been infringed. For the most serious of offences — particularly those outlined in the Criminal Code — the prosecutor must show "beyond a reasonable doubt" that the accused did it. It's not good enough to show that the accused might have done it, or that he probably did it, or that all fingers point to him in spite of his excuses. The burden of proof in these cases is much more demanding: that there is no reasonable doubt but that he — and no one else — committed the offence. This burden is required in most instances of acts considered "criminal," signifying that society views such transgressions as being very serious, and conviction should not occur lightly.

For other laws, other standards of proof are used. One alternative is the "balance of probabilities," which permits a judge to add up all the arguments, weigh them and arrive at a conclusion of what probably happened. This burden of proof is most frequently used to settle disputes between civilians — in small claims court for instance — but is also used in some "criminal" matters.

But this is the conundrum: What can be defined as criminal? There appear to be two kinds of laws. One deals with maintaining social order by specifying ground rules, or rules of the road. The other deals with matters that threaten the social order in a direct sense. The latter are laws that define criminal acts.

In his book *The Limits of the Criminal Sanction*, Herbert Packer struggles to illuminate this dilemma.

He suggests the following criteria for invoking the criminal sanction.[14]

- The conduct is prominent in most people's view of socially threatening behaviour, and is not condoned by any significant segment of society.
- Subjecting it to the criminal sanction is not inconsistent with the goals of punishment, that is, it will help to prevent crime and/or the punishment will be inflicted on the evil doers.
- Suppressing it will not inhibit socially desirable conduct.
- It may be dealt with through even-handed and non-discriminatory enforcement.
- There are no reasonable alternatives to the criminal sanction for dealing with it.

This relatively sophisticated approach should be compared with a pedestrian view more commonly held in the criminal justice system:

> The main purpose of the criminal law is to protect the law abiding members of the community from crime, making the community a safe place to live and work. Related aims of the criminal law are to alert the community and sharpen its sense of right and wrong, lawful and unlawful; to satisfy the community's sense of retribution at a level commensurate with the ideas of justice rather than with the aims of socialized vengeance; and to protect the community and heighten its feeling of security by incarcerating violent and dangerous offenders convicted of serious crimes. An additional goal of criminal law and its legal processes is to avoid the conviction of innocent persons accused of crime.[15]

This view pits the good against the bad as though there is an easy distinction between them. It casts a stern moral tone on all human activity and summons up an ill-defined public good that the criminal justice system will somehow defend. Because of its broad sweep and immediate appeal, this approach is most readily accepted by those in the best position to define right and wrong. This view dispenses with allusions to a natural standard for laws and the influence society might have on behaviour. Criminal law exists to protect the "law-abiding" members of society.

Of course, it is not easy to arrive at a definition of criminal law that is both simple and generally applicable. Criminal law seems to embody a bundle of ideas about good and bad, safety, justice, freedom, social responsibility and the deterrence of certain actions. There is general agreement that some actions are criminal in nature (for instance, a killing in cold blood), but there is no consensus in respect to activities at the edges, where individual responsibilities are weighed against societal ones (the mercy killing of a family member very ill and in great pain).

Even after a satisfactory definition is arrived at, there still remains the question why some individuals commit criminal acts and others do not. This question can be looked at on both an individual and social basis. There are four social factors that might push behaviour in a criminal direction:

- *Economic conditions*: Since Plato's day, many have suggested that poverty breeds crime, although arriving at the exact meaning of poverty in aid of this explanation is difficult. Nor is it easy to define why some people in poverty become enmeshed in crime and others do not. For every criminal born in the slums there seems to be a Horatio Alger. Some studies have shown that the rise in crime is less marked than the decline in prosperity, and that increased prosperity does not mean less crime. One refinement — suggested by the nineteenth-century Italian criminologist Filippo Poletti — attempts to relate criminal activity to all social activity, showing that the former is a percentage of the latter: more prosperity leads to more transactions, and if crime goes up as prosperity increases, the increase is in absolute numbers, not in relative terms.

Unfortunately, this comparison is almost impossible to make in real terms because of problems in collecting data. Thus, it is not known if indeed there is a relatively constant factor defining the relationship of criminal/non-criminal activity. The links between economic status, economic activity and criminal behaviour are unclear, even though we often assume that youth in the ghetto will easily turn to delinquency and crime.

- *Social conflict*: Some believe that in times of rapid change, as social controls break down, the weak are bullied by the strong — crime increases. Thus, immigrants who may have yet to establish a recognized social hierarchy may be susceptible to crime until appropriate social controls are established. The existence of the Mafia or Cosa Nostra is explained this way. While this theory can account for large criminal organizations and for riots that result in the laying of many criminal charges, it does not indicate why the majority of immigrants do not turn to crime.

- *Anomie*: The diminishing respect for authority — anomie — has been defined by existentialist thinkers like Albert Camus in *L'Étranger*. It has also been suggested as one reasonable explanation of criminal behaviour. One could say that a criminal is "alienated" from society, and his or her alienation results in crime. Thus the child from the broken home becomes a criminal thanks to alienation. Yet experience shows that the most alienated are not the most criminal (more often they become artists), and save for their illegal behaviour, many criminals appear to be socially well adjusted. Anomie can be used as an explanation of vandalism, but not of crimes involving careful planning for financial rewards — such as fraud.

- *Differential association*: The theory of differential association enunciated by Edwin Sutherland works on a balance of influences. A person subject to many bad influences and few good ones will probably end up rotten. But life is so complex that it is virtually impossible to pinpoint all one's influences, and then rank them by importance. The differential association theory becomes self-fulfilling: the analysis starts at the act complained of and works backward until the cause is discovered.

The pressure of large social forces has yet to be shown as a comprehensive explanation for crime. These grand theories explain only some actions, which is why other interpretations relate to the individual rather than society as a whole.

In fact, in the last century, criminal law has moved to a greater recognition of the role of individual factors. For instance, the M'Naghten rule, which emerged in nineteenth-century case law, states that a criminal must know the nature and the quality of the act, and know that the act is wrong, before a finding of guilt can be made. There are a number of lines of thinking that examine criminal activity on an individual basis:

- *Chemical problems*: A host of theories arose in the nineteenth century that attempted to relate criminal activities to chemical imbalances in the glands, the hormones or the blood. Some related crime to alcohol and drugs, others (in the twentieth century) to an extra male chromosome. Yet none of these rationales consistently stand up. They explain some crimes some of the time, but not much more. For instance, a heavy drug user might steal to raise drug money — but the drugs no more "caused" the crime than did the stereo set that was stolen. One recent Danish study has shown that children have criminal records much closer to their natural fathers than to adopted fathers — which might add credence to the chemical hypothesis.

- *Shape and appearance*: Theories that criminals have heads of a certain shape and faces of a certain appearance have been in vogue at various times over the last hundred years, as has the notion that criminals have a precise body shape. These ideas have become generally discredited, since there are too many criminals whose characteristics don't conform to favoured patterns.

- *Emotions*: Some hold that criminals are more aggressive — that is, more assertive, quicker to anger — than other individuals. Studies show that some criminals are indeed more aggressive than other people, but at the same time, some are less so. Others hold that criminals are psychopaths — a catch-all term — and their emotional makeup, although difficult to define precisely, results in criminal behaviour. Radzinowicz cites one critic who suggests that "a psychopath is someone we don't understand and can't treat," indicating the difficulty involved in applying this theory comprehensively.

- *The mind*: The thought that criminals have an inferior intelligence does not hold up to reasonable scrutiny; the idea that criminals have abnormal brainwaves appears to apply only to a small minority (it also applies to some non-criminals). It seems that little distinguishes the mind of a criminal from the mind of an ordinary person.

Is there anything to choose from in these theories? Some hold some truth in individual cases, but on their own, none permit one to predict criminal behaviour. They are, at best, after-the-fact explanations applied on an ad hoc basis. Just as it is difficult to define crime, it is difficult to predict who will commit crimes and understand why they acted as they did. These theories confirm our urge to explain crime but fail to provide satisfying answers. Yet if society is unclear why crime occurs, then what can be done to prevent it? What should be done with criminals?

Deterring Criminal Behaviour

A great deal of energy is devoted to deterring crime. Signs advise people not to shoplift. Police patrol endlessly to deter individuals from crime. Punishment follows a finding of a criminal intent, in the hope that others will be deterred. Does any of it matter?

There are four kinds of deterrence:

- conscience, which warns one away from certain acts for a whole host of reasons;
- the fear of detection and of the social disapproval that will follow;

- the fear of being punished; and
- the severity of the punishment itself.

What deters whom is a very complicated question, since the four factors are so intertwined. The law-abiding might be repelled by crime itself — conscience says that it is wrong — whereas another might withhold action simply because of a fear that enforcers are watching. Does an individual with a guilty conscience fear detection more than others?

Fear of detection is considered the most significant deterrent to criminal action. Thus, public police forces spend a majority of their budgets on patrol work, where officers tour in cars or on foot, providing a police presence for the purpose of deterring criminal behaviour. Private police forces are retained in growing numbers to watch over people on mass private property (this will be discussed further in chapter 3). A Kansas City study appears to cast doubt on the deterrent value of these actions,[16] but in contrast, the placement of police officers on New York's subway system seems to have been a success.

There is a widely expressed feeling that punishments should be made more severe to act as a deterrent to murder (offenders should be killed by the state) and violent crimes (offenders should be incarcerated for longer terms). In fact, this outcry probably is also inspired by revenge and retribution as well as deterrence. Studies in Canada and elsewhere have indicated that at least in regard to murder, reducing the severity of the punishment by removing the option of capital punishment has not increased the rate of offences. Thus, there are serious questions as to how effective a deterrent severe punishment really is.

American sociologist James Q. Wilson argues that

severity of punishment may indeed affect crime rates, but that the issue is fraught with difficulties, as is apparent from his recent writing:

> I believe that the weight of the evidence — aggregate statistical analyses, evaluations of experiments and quasi-experiments, and studies of individual behaviour — supports the view that the rate of crime is influenced by its costs. This influence is greater — or easier to observe — for some crimes and persons than for others. The crime rate can be lowered by increasing the certainty of sanctions, but inducing the criminal-justice system to make those changes is difficult, especially if apprehending and punishing the offender is not rewarding to members of the criminal-justice system, or if the crime lacks the strong moral condemnation of society....Despite the uncertainty that attaches to the connection between the economy and crime, I believe that the wisest course of action for society is to try to increase the benefits of non-criminal behaviour and the costs of crime simultaneously, all the while bearing in mind that no feasible change in either part of the equation is likely to produce big changes in crime rates.[17]

The sticky problem of assessing the value of deterrents is a result of the difficulty in actually defining crime, and accounting for why it occurs. It may be that money now spent on punishment (particularly the astronomical costs of incarceration) might better be spent spreading shared social values, to influence the idea of conscience. Police officers and social workers display this belief when they establish boxing and other athletic clubs for youths, community centres, and other places of recreation where younger people can learn appropriate social values (as well as being kept "off the street,'' where they might learn ''unacceptable'' values).

Wilson neatly summarizes the hopes and fears of this approach:

> If criminals are rational people like the rest of us, then it stands to reason that temperament and family experiences, which most shape values, will have the greatest effect on crime, and that perceived costs and benefits will have a lesser effect....
>
> In a sense the radical critics of America are correct. If you wish to make a big difference in crime rates, you must make a fundamental change in society. But what they propose to put in place of existing institutions, to the extent that they propose anything at all except angry rhetoric, would leave us yearning for the good old days when our crime rate may have been higher but our freedom intact.

Perhaps ideas of successful deterrents flow directly from one's definition of crime, as discussed earlier in this chapter. Those who argue that severe punishment is the best deterrent don't acknowledge the great perceptual and experimental problems in this area of human behaviour. As is argued in the next section, a great deal of criminal behaviour does not even come to public attention, making a mockery of the notion that severe punishments will deter the ne'er-do-well.

The Dark Figure of Crime and the Criminal Justice System

Earlier in this chapter we saw that official statistics suggested the fear of crime has outstripped actual occurrences. But can we rely on police figures for an accurate portrait of crime? The image is blurred by the dark figure of crime — crime that is hidden. There is a gap between the actual number of incidents and those recorded as criminal acts.[18] The gap is substantial: it varies depending on the offence and is augmented in a most frightening way by the public perception of pervasive crime.

The most serious of crimes — murder — gives a fair indication of how profound this mystery is. Cases abound of murderers who, when apprehended, spill out stories of many homicides that the police were unaware of. Some murders are hidden away in families; some are disguised as accidents; some never come to light, as victims (particularly rootless youths) disappear in unclear circumstances. A generally agreed-upon estimate is that for every murder known to authorities, another three or four are never reported. Some writers put the ratio at one to nine.

By their nature, certain crimes are invisible to the police. The parties involved have no reason to reveal that an abortion is being performed in jurisdictions where such an act is illegal. The same is true of gambling. Theft in the workplace is often resolved between the employer and employee without reference to police. Many shoplifters are not turned over to the police. In some situations, government authorities themselves attempt to hide criminal activity, as in the classic American example of Watergate.

There are many reasons why people decide not to report criminal activity, thus depriving officials of an accurate sense of crime rates. The following reasons are given for not reporting incidents:

- The police wouldn't have done anything about the incident, even if it were reported.
- The offender would probably never have been

caught.

- Reporting the incident would have cost the complainant time and trouble going to the station, making a statement, identifying the suspect and going to court.
- The incident was considered to be a private matter (such as a family fight) in which police intervention was not welcome.
- A private settlement was worked out, such as reparation, replacement of stolen goods, agreeing to quit one's job for stealing at work.
- The complainant was personally involved in the incident (having received stolen goods, for instance) and thus stood to lose by reporting it to the police.
- People don't like being tattletales and fear the consequences if it becomes known that they complained.
- The complainant fears that police will not believe the story, particularly if it involves rape or lost property.

It is generally thought that only three or four out of every one hundred occurrences come to the attention of the police in Western society. One estimate is broken down in the following way:[19]

	Unreported Incidents	Reported Crimes
Rape, indecent assault	10	1
Homicides	3-6	1
Frauds	8	1
Thefts, robberies	1	1

There is another manner in which crime can go unnoticed — as a result of police action. In some

situations, police decide to give a warning rather than
lay a charge or fill out a formal occurrence report. In
either situation, the incident does not become part of
crime statistics. Further, in order to improve the clearance rate, police might decide not to report certain
occurrences that are judged to be unresolvable. Lastly,
not all charges laid result in a conviction.

Thus, there is a substantial attrition rate in the criminal justice system. The federal solicitor general reports
that of all break and enters in the 1970s (as estimated
from victim surveys), 60 per cent are reported to police,
10 per cent result in a charge, and less than 6 per cent
lead to a conviction.[20]

The Canadian justice system is not one where
offenders keep dropping through holes from ineffi-
ciency. All Western justice systems seem to work this
way. By reviewing participants' accounts of crimes
unknown to the police, Radzinowicz arrived at this
rule of thumb for Western countries: one-quarter of
all crime comes to the attention of police. If charges
are laid in one-fifth of these, about 5 per cent of *all*
criminal incidents result in a charge. The police can
do nothing about offences that do not come to their
attention. Of those they know about, charges can only
be laid if there are adequate grounds to believe that a
case can be made in court. A judge cannot register a
conviction unless he is convinced beyond a reasonable
doubt that the accused committed the offence (and if
the accused has not been able to discover a technical
defence).

New York City provides a good example. In 1980,
520,000 incidents led to 16,000 arrests and 5,000
convictions. Of those convicted, 2,000 were sent to
jail. In the remainder of convictions, judges chose
dispositions including absolute discharge, fines, parole

and community service. It seems generally agreed that incarceration solves few problems and is exceedingly expensive (one estimate says that the penitentiary staff in Canada is as large as those imprisoned there),[21] and is not responding to the high rates of recidivism.

Against these figures of reported and unreported crime, it is helpful to set numbers regarding police strength. In 1980 the total strength of all public police forces in Canada was 54,424, of which slightly more than 18 per cent were civilian personnel. Of the total force, 5 per cent were federal, 29 per cent provincial, and 66 per cent municipal. The bulk of policing is at the local level. Total police expenditure in 1980 amounted to $1.7 billion, far beyond the $200 million laid out in 1962. Real-dollar increase in the decade 1970 to 1980 was about 15 per cent.

There are approximately 1.8 million Criminal Code offences that come to the attention of police every year. Thus, on a very rough average each officer deals with thirty-one offences a year, or one about every ten days. As can be easily calculated by comparing the number of officers with the data presented in the first part of this chapter, an officer can expect to deal with an average of less than three offences involving violence a year.

The scope of the dark figure of crime raises important questions. The true composition of criminal activity (and of the criminal population), as well as its present trends, is unknown and can only be guessed at. It seems that society's expectation — that police stamp out crime — is unrealistic, since even now we are neither catching nor punishing the vast majority of criminals. Yet the consequences of a drive to apprehend more suspects are worrisome. The justice system would be unable to handle the sheer numbers of people, and would collapse under the weight of more charges and trials. New jails would be required — the existing ones are full. The costs of more prosecutions and more convictions — entailing more judges, more prosecutors, more courtrooms, more parole officers, and on and on — would be significant, and would spark a public outcry. Perhaps society is better off attempting to catch a representative sample of criminals. But what is representative of real crime? This central question comes back to haunt us.

Organized Crime

That identifying the true criminal and apprehending him or her are mighty challenges is nowhere clearer than in the sphere of organized crime. For the public, there is probably no police problem more intriguing than this area of criminality. Society gobbles up every morsel of news about gang killings, giant scams, numbers rackets and drug deals, and just as readily looks to the police to put an end to all this fascinating activity. The exotic world of organized crime seems set apart from the rest of society, operating with its own set of values and order.

The idea of organized crime — that is, people acting in concert for criminal purposes — is not new. In Elizabethan England large groups were involved in banditry and piracy, and as cities grew larger and more industrialized, organizations devoted to crime created a home for themselves in the midst of urban society.

In a remarkable book, *Organized Crime and Criminal Organization,* D.R. Cressey identifies six levels of organized crime distinguished by degree of sophistication and intensity of the conspirators' involvement. They are:[22]

- *The amateurs*: Two or more people agree to engage in the simplest of criminal acts — breaking into a home or stealing a few apples from a grocer. There is no specialization and almost no planning. Examples are kids on a spree, or two people deciding on the spur of the moment to carry out a mugging or a rape.

- *The tacticians*: Here participants use their individual skills to best advantage. Specialists might be engaged (for instance, to break the code on a vault or to deactivate an alarm system). Some sense of tactics is involved. An example is thieves who pick a target by combing newspaper death notices to find a household that will be emptied for a funeral.

- *The strategists*: Those falling under this rubric look at crime in a sophisticated way. The criminals involved are not only specialists, but they select crimes they are likely to get away with because of public indifference or because victims will not complain too loudly. This might involve stolen goods, where victims are inconvenienced but suffer little financial loss thanks to insurance. A classic example was the ''Great Train Robbery'' in Great Britain in the mid-1960s: members of that group were seen by some as heroes for having made off with huge sums of money, without causing physical harm. The thieves managed to elude police for more than a decade.

- *The corruptors*: Some forms of crime draw in people on the fringes, people not directly involved in the commission of the crime, but who play a supporting role that ensures success. Those who are corrupted receive a benefit for their part. The most common example of this kind of organized crime involves government officials misusing permissive powers:

the police officer who for a price agrees not to enforce certain laws, or a government official who receives money for granting a licence. To reach this stage, a member of the criminal organization must of course possess the skills to corrupt someone outside the group. The group then is extended beyond its simple membership.

- *The enforcers*: It is an easy step to add an enforcer to those whose job it is to corrupt others for their mutual benefit. The enforcer makes sure the corruptee delivers. Organizing crime in this manner is quite sophisticated, since it means that people outside the group must be pressured to act in certain ways, a dangerous arrangement in any case. People must be drawn in through benefits offered (or through threats), and then kept in line with strong-arm tactics. The Fulton Fish Market in New York is controlled by an organized crime corporation which requires those who supply fish or buy wholesale to pay a user's fee to the corporation, thus corrupting them. But it also punishes those who refuse to pay by slashing tires or breaking truck windows — thus enforcing the powers of corruption.

- *The corporation*: The most sophisticated way of organizing crime is by using a corporate model to structure the members in the group. This is the model most often referred to when the Mafia or the Cosa Nostra is discussed. The corporation includes the activities of the other models, embodying tacticians, strategists, corruptors and enforcers. What makes it different is its permanence, the same kind of permanence one finds with any other corporation. These corporations are usually called "families," even though blood relationships are weaker than in most family-run businesses in the legitimate world. These corporations usually have known products and services — drugs, prostitution, loansharking and so forth — as well as a specific territory, and corporations are known to compete with each other (often quite violently) for territory or products.

The latter model, the ultimate level of organized crime, has other similarities to a traditional corporation. At the top of the pyramid is a company president, often referred to as ''boss,'' under whom are arranged vice presidents with responsibilities for certain product lines, territories or procedures. These vice presidents are called ''sottocaps,'' an Italian term connoting second in command. Further down the line are managers of various divisions (''lieutenants''), overseeing the workers (or ''soldiers''). The corporation has a clear structure, with direct lines of responsibility, and thus changes of personnel and threats to business can be managed in an organized fashion. The remarkable feature of the corporation is its ability to deal routinely with most of the pressures it is likely to face. This is as true for a company selling pharmaceuticals as it is for one dealing in prostitution or protection.

The major difference between a corporation involved in crime and one involved in legitimate activities is that the former is not registered with the government, and is not eager or able to talk about its internal structure. This structure is characterized by a certain looseness: there is usually a buffer between the president and the vice presidents so that it is difficult to trace lines of command and flows of money. Those gaps are often filled by legal advisors. These lawyers enjoy a general immunity from prosecution (because of the cloak of client/solicitor privilege they can attach to consultations with the corporation), which shields their clients from the prying eyes of police and the courts. Corporate looseness is not a mark of weak organization — it is simply an operating strategy.

Most individuals in the crime corporation have a very specific job related to the enterprise. The one exception is the enforcer: this task is carried out from time to time by different individuals, making it difficult to know exactly who will enforce company directives. In this area, surprise seems quite effective.

The corporation protects its members, providing they adhere to the rule of *"omerta"* (a Sicilian term meaning never to speak badly of anyone). The rule requires that if a member of a crime corporation is apprehended by police or a rival corporation, he must remain silent and not disclose the business of the corporation. If *omerta* is observed, the corporation will support the individual's family while he is in jail. If *omerta* is not observed, the family will not be protected and indeed might be subject to physical harm. There is a strong inducement to be silent.

There is a widespread belief that these corporations are populated by people of Italian parentage. Many are. A common ethnic bond both encourages cohesion and helps sort out problems of succession. But individuals of all nationalities are involved in crime corporations. As for the "ethnics," one thought is that some immigrant groups predominate in some crime corporations because they were shut out of traditional endeavours by the social and economic elite of the day. The immigrants decided to pursue the only business opportunities they could find — criminal ones.

The business of crime corporations is extensive. Endeavours include: labour racketeering (for instance, gaining control of a union and then making tough demands on employers, as has happened with the

Teamsters in the United States); cargo thefts; fencing or trading in stolen goods; gambling; loansharking or loaning money to people literally on the security of their body, often charging very high interest rates; the drug trade; political corruption; arson (for insurance fraud); extortion; and many more. The corporations operate as illegal cartels and are often large enough to function like unofficial governments. The availability of deep wells of capital means illegitimate companies can easily buy legitimate ones, as indeed they have. In some cases they control activities very important to the life of a city. The Fulton Fish Market in New York City, mentioned earlier, has revenues of three-quarters of a billion dollars annually.

The size and nature of crime corporations in Canada were put succinctly in 1975 by Jean Dutil, chairman of the Inquiry into Organized Crime in Quebec:

> …organized crime costs at least 10% of provincial taxes, plus between 25 cents and a dollar a day for every Quebecer. Organized criminals have passed beyond the stage of "buying" politicians and policemen, although they still do if they find it possible and profitable, and have infiltrated legitimate business. Profits for such illegal activities as prostitution, gambling, drug trafficking and loansharking are invested in such legitimate businesses as food and furniture industries and sanitary services. The cost of organized crime to the consumer stems from the tribute paid by organized criminals somewhere in the chain of production to the consumption of goods and services….
>
> …the profits of organized crime in Quebec are in excess of $800 million annually, and if organized criminals paid taxes on their illegal gains all Quebec taxes could be reduced by 10%….The profits of various categories of crime [are] as follows: counterfeiting $1

million; fraud $20 million; drug trafficking $60 million; protection and extortion $5 million; illegal games and bookmaking $2.5 million. All these profits are small...when compared with the "gigantic revenues" made from loansharking, which has an average turnover of $800 million with an average interest rate of 400%.[23]

There is no reason to believe that the extent of crime corporations is any greater in Quebec than elsewhere in Canada, nor that the problem has eased since 1976. In fact, many feel that it has grown in the interim. Most provinces have been concerned enough to publish information and convene commissions of inquiry into organized crime.

But crime corporations are extremely resilient. Other forms of organized crime — such as a bank holdup ring — can be broken up by arresting the ringleaders. But in the corporation, individuals are subservient to the whole. Vacancies are easily filled. The only doubt concerns the ability of certain individuals to perform certain tasks in a satisfactory (or imaginative) manner.

Thus, the loss by arrest of a middle manager causes but a moment's difficulty for the crime corporation. Because of the strength of *omerta*, the arrest is unlikely to produce information helpful to police. And it is difficult for the police to bring in senior management because of the buffers that break a provable chain of command. Workers or soldiers can be arrested, but even if they talk, the information will reflect only their minor role in the workings of the corporation. Consequently, the crime corporation is impervious to traditional policing methods.

When the rare significant arrest is made, the crime corporation goes to extraordinary lengths to protect itself and its senior personnel. The example of Paul, Albert and Eugene Volpe, who with one other person were charged in 1965 with conspiracy to extort money from a Toronto businessman, is instructive. During the first trial, a juror stood up and said that he could not follow the evidence because of language difficulties. This led to a mistrial. At the second trial, one of the twelve jurors insisted on a not-guilty verdict for no apparent reason. The third trial was ended when a friend of the Volpes was caught trying to bribe a juror. At the fourth trial, the jury found the Volpes not guilty, and the case was appealed to the Supreme Court of Canada. The Supreme Court held that the judge had misdirected the jury, and a fifth trial was ordered. Plea bargaining then began, in which two of the accused agreed to plead guilty to (lesser) charges of conspiracy to obtain money by threat, providing the extortion charges were dropped. Paul Volpe was sentenced to two years in jail, Eugene Volpe to three months. Albert Volpe skipped the country, not to return until 1971, by which time the businessman had left Toronto and refused to return to give evidence. The charges were dropped.[24]

Obviously, the criminal justice system has great trouble coping with those who put up such a fight. The system is much better at dealing with simple events and with accused persons who are contrite rather than combative. The idea that criminals are much like ordinary businessmen and that crime might be carried on by an organization that exists for that purpose, does not fit easily within present perceptions about criminal justice. Thus, effective action against the crime corporation is most difficult.

Provincial and national policing organizations cooperate in their actions against crime corporations. They share information (in Ontario the larger forces are linked together to analyze data and identify senior members of crime corporations) and take joint action, sometimes involving the RCMP. Police colleges offer courses on appropriate investigative techniques.

But this is not enough. It is generally agreed that effective action requires the appointment of a special police team that is responsible for investigation and prosecution. Vancouver has such a team, known as CLEU (Criminal Law Enforcement Unit), which includes lawyers who sift through evidence. The process is lengthy and tedious, beginning with a careful analysis of information at hand, going on to targeting of specific individuals, systematic surveillance, meticulous preparation of cases, and, finally, prosecution. It is expensive and time-consuming, more so if the accused puts up a fight and necessitates multiple trials, as in the Volpe case.

Even when prosecution results in the incarceration of an individual, the police face the fact that the crime corporation continues to flourish, with the role of the accused being filled by someone else. This is very discouraging. For society, there is considerable question whether police action has any real effect on the operation of crime corporations. The best the police can do might be nothing more than a small nettle in the transactions of a crime empire.

In light of this, two general approaches have been suggested to confront crime corporations. One is to legitimize some of the activities they now control. Some advocate legalizing certain narcotics so as to end organized crime's distribution monopoly in the drug trade. Others urge lifting the legal taboos against gambling and prostitution to the same effect. Yet this approach will hardly stem the tide. Crime corporations are willing to do what other enterprises are not: to lend money on no security, for instance. Most of the activities of crime corporations are those society would never wish to legitimize.

A second strategy is to devise laws that prohibit individual involvement in a crime corporation. These laws would see crime as a product of individuals working together, rather than resulting from an individual acting alone — the traditional view. The *organization* of gambling, prostitution and drug distribution would specifically be made a crime. Crime corporations would then be considered illegitimate, and criminal in nature.

Various American jurisdictions have struggled with this approach. The return appears to be small. Police continue to be faced with *omertà*, and those under surveillance are probably more technologically sophisticated than the police, and so can avoid detection. In any event, it is difficult to define exactly what is meant by "organized crime," since crime corporations are increasingly interwoven with legitimate enterprises that often mask a criminal presence.

Perhaps crime corporations are simply too big, powerful and determined for the police and our delicate criminal justice system. Crime corporations should be viewed as alternative kinds of government that attempt to usurp the freedoms and relationships that have evolved in society. A helpful analogy may be with pornography (which is a growth industry for crime corporations). Pornography is of concern to many because it represents a disturbing shift in values and appears to be pervasive. While most people want to maintain freedom of the press and "freedom to read," and also believe an interest in sex is natural, they sense pornography has an evil edge to it, debasing sexual relations and perverting human relations as a whole.

While it is difficult to define the exact limits of what society considers acceptable, many recognize that at some point on the continuum, pornography has to be controlled.

It is the same with the crime organization. Organizations involved in drug dealing and the like are worrisome — yet they feed a public appetite that will not disappear. Like pornography, they seem to defy easy definition and response, even though society recognizes them as undesirable.

This chapter has moved from a statistical picture of crime, through the difficult questions of who the criminals are and how to define crime, to the idea of deterrence. The images of crime rates one gains from official statistics and estimates of "the dark figure of crime" are contradictory — but in their divergence they both point to the fact that crime, the wellspring of public expectations for the police, is only very dimly understood. And reviewing organized crime has shown that crime can be much more sinister than the actions of certain individuals — it can be a dominant way of life.

It is within this context that police find a role for themselves, a role that plays on widely held fears of criminal activity to shape a public presence. We now turn to the police response to crime to discover how their work is structured and what it is they actually do.

3
The Structure of Policing

Police personnel are organized specifically to fight crime, even though that activity represents a small part of their total workload. This organizational framework is apparent in the formal structure of a particular force and in the elements shaping an officer's work, like recruitment, training, discipline, and police unionism. This chapter looks at these issues and closes by contrasting the work of public police with that of private policing agencies.

The organizations that police different Canadian cities are similar in terms of shape and scope of operation. While the RCMP polices a small town in British Columbia differently than a municipally controlled force polices a large urban centre, the twenty-five largest urban areas in Canada show a marked consistency in how their forces are structured, the way they attract new members, and how they go about day-to-day operations.[1]

The modern police force has three main elements:

- administration — handling the functions required to keep a large bureaucracy afloat;
- field operations — including patrol, traffic and other general activities; and
- staff operations — the more-specialized services, such as the holdup squad, homicide, youth, morality and so forth.

Figures 3-1 and 3-2 (pages 80-81) are organizational charts for forces in Calgary and Ottawa. They are typical of the structure of large forces. What differences do exist are confined to the names given to units carrying out similar functions. The structure is hierarchical, with units broken down by function (for example, the criminal investigation divisions), or geographical (as in field operations).

The charts do not show how the bulk of manpower is located in patrol work. For this we must turn to staff allocations and expenditures. The Metro Toronto police force provides a representative picture: 75 per cent of the total budget is devoted to field operations, and of that, more than half is for patrol.

The following breakdown of the Metro Toronto force indicates how manpower is deployed in a large force in 1984.

Unit and Function	Expenditure ($millions)	Personnel Uniform	Civilian
Administration	48.3	186	493
Recruitment and training		110	
Staff Operations	47.9	589	702
Intelligence		125	17
Morality		64	7
Internal affairs		8	1
Complaints		20	3
Planning and research		2	6
Other	12.68		26
Homicide		25	1
Investigative support		33	1
Auto recovery		32	2
Holdup		20	1
Fraud and forgery		33	3
Bail and parole		6	4
Identification		50	52

Unit and Function	Expenditure ($millions)	Personnel Uniform	Civilian
Communications		66	185
Summons		37	141
Court		53	138
Vehicle maintenance		-	110
Youth Bureau		15	6
Marine unit		38	5
Other		7	4
Field Operations	203.5	4,584	450
Youth workers		106	
Foot patrol		320	
Mobile patrol		2,434	
Patrol support		339	
Detectives		582	
Community relations		58	
Traffic		310	
Crime prevention		31	
Mounted police		79	
Emergency Task Force		79	
Ethnic and community services		21	
Parking control officers			136

There are some surprises in this allocation. The number of officers assigned to deal with youth is less than the number involved in intelligence (''to monitor organized crime and report major crime activities directly to the chief''). There are many more officers in the mounted squad than in the ethnic and community branch, a considerable anomaly given the attention the police say is paid to the many minority and ethnic groups in the city. Only a handful of officers is directly engaged in crime prevention.

The bulk of the force is engaged in foot and mobile (that is, vehicular) patrol, backed up by detectives who

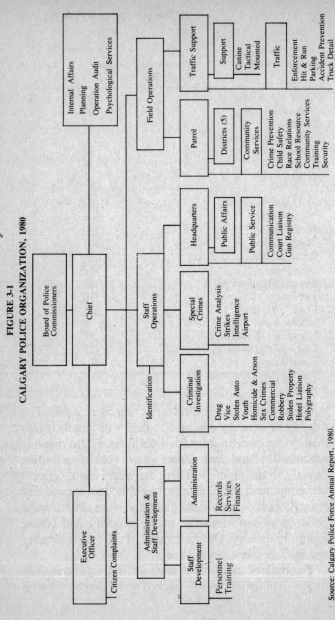

FIGURE 3-1

CALGARY POLICE ORGANIZATION, 1980

Source: Calgary Police Force Annual Report, 1980.

FIGURE 3-2
OTTAWA POLICE FORCE ORGANIZATION, CA. 1976

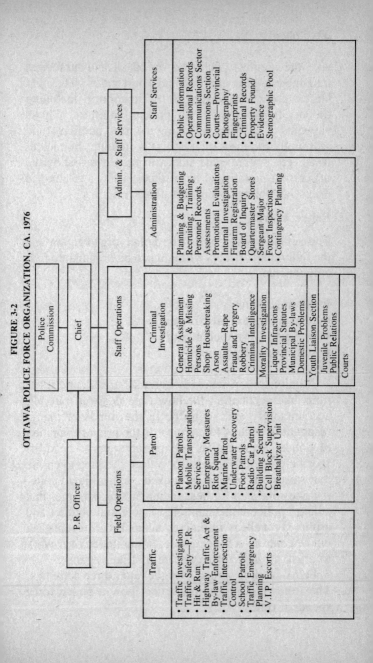

Police Commission

Chief

P.R. Officer

Staff Operations

Criminal Investigation
- General Assignment
- Homicide & Missing Persons
- Shop/ Housebreaking
- Arson
- Assaults—Rape
- Fraud and Forgery
- Robbery
- Criminal Intelligence
- Morality Investigation
- Liquor Infractions
- Provincial Statutes
- Municipal By-laws
- Domestic Problems
- Youth Liaison Section
- Juvenile Problems
- Public Relations
- Courts

Admin. & Staff Services

Administration
- Planning & Budgeting
- Recruiting, Training, Personnel Records, Assessments
- Promotional Evaluations
- Internal Investigation
- Firearm Registration
- Board of Inquiry
- Quartermaster Stores
- Sergeant Major
- Force Inspections
- Contingency Planning

Staff Services
- Public Information
- Operational Records
- Communications Sector
- Summons Section
- Courts—Provincial
- Photography/ Fingerprints
- Criminal Records
- Property Found/ Evidence
- Stenographic Pool

Field Operations

Patrol
- Platoon Patrols
- Mobile Transportation Service
- Emergency Measures
- Riot Squad
- Marine Patrol
- Underwater Recovery
- Foot Patrols
- Radio Car Patrol
- Building Security
- Cell Block Supervision
- Breathalyzer Unit

Traffic
- Traffic Investigation
- Traffic Safety—P.R.
- Hit & Run
- Highway Traffic Act & By-law Enforcement
- Traffic Intersection Control
- School Patrols
- Traffic Emergency Planning
- V.I.P. Escorts

take the incidents gathered on patrol and turn them into material for charges and court cases. The next largest group is involved in traffic control, including the civilians engaged in parking matters. Those elements of the force receiving the most publicity (and seemingly the most interesting) — holdup, homicide, fraud, etc. — are quite small, in fact, dwarfed by the officers in morality ("to enforce the laws relating to drugs, gambling and prostitution").

Police Work

The actual work done by the police organization and the individual officers within it can be broken into four components:

- administration:
- responding to calls for service;
- preventative policing; and
- self-initiated policing.

Administration involves normal bureaucratic functions like accounting for how time is spent, payroll, accountability and so forth. In the minds of many, responding to calls for service is the primary function of police. Preventative policing attempts to head off specific crimes, as in a patrol officer checking to ensure that stores are adequately locked. Self-initiated policing goes one step further, encompassing activities that enlarge police understanding of potential conflict and crime, as well as initiatives taken before events get out of control — for example, doing undercover work to crack a robbery ring before it strikes again.

Patrol work is spread over the latter three activities. The following allocations reflect how a police force spends it time:[2]

Administration	23 per cent
Calls for service	23 per cent
Preventative policing	40 per cent
Self-initiated policing	14 per cent

Much public attention is directed to response for calls, and forces in turn take pride in their ability to respond quickly. Often the first note sounded by senior officers when confronted with budget cuts is that response times will deteriorate.

However, the assumption that a speedy response is the *sine qua non* of policing may be ill-founded. A study in Kansas City in the early 1970s showed that considerable time elapsed between an incident and a call to police for aid. Dividing the time elapsed between a robbery and the arrival of the police into 100 units, the study found that 84 units elapsed prior to a call to police, 7 units elapsed during the communication interval, and 9 units elapsed until the police arrived.[3]

Apparently the first response of victims is not to call the police for help but to turn to neighbours, friends and relatives for support. Would reporting intervals be even longer for incidents in which there is no personal violence?

One analyst argues that immediate responses are required in only a small percentage of calls, and suggests the following guide:[4]

- 10 per cent require an immediate response, since an occurrence is in progress;
- 30 per cent require a response to an event that has happened and attendance should be soon; and
- 60 per cent probably don't require a response at all — they can be dealt with on the telephone.

One study concludes that the critical question is when the complainant *expects* the police to arrive.[5] If the police are expected in sixty minutes, an arrival then is as good to the complainant as an appearance in ten minutes. The aggravation occurs when police are expected immediately but do not appear for an hour or more. Many Canadian forces are now experimenting with screening calls to determine which ones require priority and haste.

The emergency "911" telephone systems being established across Canada are based on the assumption that there should be a central hot line for speedy police, fire and ambulance service. The system permits the emergency service to "hold" callers so that their location can be pinpointed if they are incoherent or creating a false alarm. While the "hold" capability may be valuable in life-and-death situations, requiring ambulance and fire-fighting services, the centralized rapid response system bears little relation to police functions. It is ironic that 911 systems are generally being established as adjuncts of police operations.

There can be no doubt that the radio has influenced the way police work is perceived both by officers and the public. The radio provides the instant communication that aids (or feeds) a speedy response syndrome. As one author notes:

> When it was introduced, [the radio] was heralded by many as the long-awaited technological breakthrough that would allow the police to dampen, if not extinguish, crime. Of course…neither the radio system nor any other technological innovation has had a demonstrable effect on the level of crime. However, it has had a definite effect on the organization of patrol work, enabling mobile officers to receive requests for their presence on a perpetual basis. This in turn has

affected the way people mobilize police…it has probably also affected their willingness to call police (because of their availability) and the types of things they call them for.[6]

Today, as officers are being taken out of patrol cars and put on foot patrol, they are still equipped with sophisticated radios that provide instant access, even though the officers cannot move with corresponding speed. In Toronto an officer called to the scene of a mugging in 1982 was forced to travel by streetcar, arriving an hour after the call was received. The fact that the person assaulted was a leading black civil rights worker did not lessen the impact of the anomaly.

For the officer, the idea of a speedy response is a mixed blessing. Some officers feel they are little more than puppets of a dispatcher barking out orders.[7] One method of avoiding calls is to leave the cruiser and walk up an alley on the pretense of investigating a suspicious-looking person or situation. If an unsavoury call cannot be avoided, an officer can delay response in the hope the problem might resolve itself. Canadian criminologist Richard Ericson surveyed how officers viewed calls for service: 15 per cent of calls were considered exciting, 10 per cent boring, and the rest routine. After the calls had been responded to, only 6 per cent were judged exciting. Responding to calls for service can very easily become a tedious pastime, one that might be sparkled up with a fast drive to the destination. Like the radio, the automobile has helped define the way police do their work, in particular by reinforcing the bias to response-to-calls service.

When the modern police force was first set up in London, England, foot patrols established the image of the cop on the beat. This image persists in spite of the predominance of vehicular patrol. O.W. Wilson

— an American criminologist who became a senior police administrator — provided a three-point rationale for dependence on patrols.[8] First, by being almost everywhere at once — a police omnipresence — a force minimizes the opportunity for crime. Second, a wholesome influence is exerted as the police on their rounds reach out to people in the community. Third, constant presence provides welcome services not related to crime — helping find lost children, for example.

Questions might be raised about whether the latter two effects are produced by vehicular patrol and whether the first results from foot patrol. In any event, the worth of patrol should be judged in terms of both effectiveness and cost-efficiency. Does patrolling accomplish its goals?

In his study, Ericson notes that the actual number of proactive (or preventative) contacts per shift is relatively small — less than two times a shift an officer can expect to "reach out" to those he meets on patrol.[9] Further, such proactive stops are responsible for very few charges. Even in situations where an officer stops another vehicle, offences are recorded in only 40 per cent of cases.[10] Ericson argues that decisions to make proactive stops often appear to be spontaneous, and related more closely to the monthly activity sheet (which virtually sets a quota for charges for various kinds of offences) than to any other factor.[11]

In his study (of the Peel Regional Police Force, which serves a suburban community of 300,000 to the west of Toronto), Ericson was able to get a reasonably full picture of what happens on a normal shift.[12] On average, an officer could expect two minor citizen contacts, that is, incidents where the dispute is brief and minor, ranging from taking a few minutes to check the occupants of a parked car to spending half an hour talking to citizens. The average is about fifteen minutes per contact.

The more serious incidents — longer and more complex encounters than citizen contacts, possibly resulting in the officer writing out an occurrence, issuing a summons or making an arrest — could be expected every second shift. This kind of incident could be expected to take forty-five minutes.

One property check — such as following up on a burglary alarm — typically occurs on every shift. The above tasks might be augmented by special duties assigned that day or court obligations, either of which would also probably come up once a shift. Last, an average of slightly more than one occurrence report would be filed per shift.

In all, Ericson can account for about two and a half hours of such activities in the normal shift. The rest of the time is spent simply being there, having a presence, creating the omnipresence endorsed by Wilson. Apparently the "reaching out" function is quite limited in reality, especially since all forms of police/citizen contact occupy less than ninety minutes per shift.

Charges laid as a result of patrol work are rare. On average, an officer in a large metropolitan force will lay several criminal charges a month, and the median figures are bound to indicate that a significant percentage of officers make no arrests in any given year. The following table compares offences per officer in three jurisdictions:

Offences per Officer, 1982

	Criminal Offences	Violent Offences
Toronto	39	2
Ottawa	64	4
Vancouver	71	8

Ericson concludes that patrol work is primarily a matter of keeping order, a tedious function:

> ...patrol officers sometimes find it appropriate to use criminal law to reproduce order. Such occasions are relatively rare, and their occurrence certainly does not indicate that the officer's primary task is criminal law enforcement. Rather, the law is occasionally invoked because it comes in handy as an enabling device to assert order. While some people are selected out and others ignored, all are reminded of the "order of things."[13]

> ...the bulk of the patrol officer's time was spent doing nothing other than consuming the petrochemical energy required to run an automobile and the psychic energy required to deal with the boredom of it all. While this work may serve to order the population, it hardly brings personal dignity to anyone involved. The question remains whether the work is worth doing with such intensity at all.[14]

The 1972 Kansas City study already referred to casts more doubt on the efficacy of "the cop on the beat."[15] Three areas were chosen for study. In one, patrols were maintained at normal levels. In another, patrols were entirely removed, and police only responded to calls for service. In the third, patrols were increased threefold. At the end of the study year, it was found that the amount or intensity of patrol work had no bearing on the level of crime, nor on the community's sense of security. Police patrols appeared to accomplish very little.

The methodology of the Kansas City study has been questioned. The area without patrol was regularly traversed by police cars in the area for other reasons, and the public perception might have been that the area was still well patrolled. The zone without patrols was long and thin, and thus the police presence in neighbouring zones might have been felt. Whether these criticisms invalidate the results of the experiment awaits further study.

One interesting facet of patrol work is the car chase. In the eighteen-month period between July 1, 1980, and December 31, 1981, there were 400 recorded police chases in Metro Toronto, or an average of one reported chase every thirty-one hours. Although police regulations require that chases be reported as they begin, it is widely thought that the actual number of chases is double the recorded one (no doubt the unreported chases are uneventful). There is no predictable length of time for a chase. Averages fall between fifteen seconds and five minutes.

Metro Toronto police give speeding as the reason for beginning almost half of all pursuits. Next in importance is failing to obey a traffic signal and failing to stop for a police officer. Eighty-four per cent of pursuits are successful in stopping the driver.

The 400 reported chases resulted in 536 criminal charges and a smaller number of Highway Traffic Act charges. Ninety-six people were injured (half civilians and half police), and property damage amounted to $280,000. On average then, personal injury occurred in every fourth chase, and the average chase caused $700 property damage.

It is difficult not to think that many police chases are a reaction to long and tedious hours of unproductive patrol work. The antidote to boredom is creating excitement. At the same time, one must recognize that some chases are a perfectly reasonable response to a given situation.

Detective Work

The function of the detective is to "investigate all criminal offences." More specifically, the detective's role is to review occurrence reports submitted by patrol officers and make those occurrences into crimes that can be processed through the criminal justice system. The patrol officer delivers the suspect and/or the victim's story to the detective, who then takes over.

Historically, the role of the detective succeeded that of the patrol officer. When modern policing began in London in 1829, all officers were uniformed; this was one of the few ways the public could be assured that the police were not acting secretly, like the dreaded gendarmes in France. The surveillance provided by police was visible. But as crime continued its rampant path apparently undeterred by the uniformed force, some officers slipped into civilian clothes to perform a new function — quietly watching criminals to discover evidence that would lead to conviction (and also catching criminals red-handed). The idea of the plain-clothes detective was born.

For all of the glamour and publicity given them in novels, movies and television, detectives are not very public figures. Their visibility is low, and much of their work on all but the most spectacular cases is done out of the limelight. This well suits the detective's job, which is putting facts together in such a way that a suspect can be found for a crime and a conviction can be registered. In this role the detective wants a free hand, not another pair of eyes peering over his shoulder.

There is a natural tension between the patrol officer and the detective. The detective louses up the case the officer thought was solid. The detective gets whatever public glory there is for punishing the culprit, while the officer receives no recognition. The officer spends his time on the street, sometimes exposed to violence, while the detective — dressed in civies — sits in his office mulling over papers.

Ericson studied the work of Peel detectives over a period of 179 shifts. He found that the workload broke down as follows:[16]

Case investigation, including interviewing complainants, witnesses and informers	22.1 per cent
Suspect investigation, including interviewing suspects and processing the accused	10.6 per cent
General patrol	2.2 per cent
Court	2.4 per cent
Office (not including case or suspect investigation)	46.4 per cent
Non-police activity	11.2 per cent
Miscellaneous	5.1 per cent

According to this data, detectives spent almost half their working hours preparing to tell their superiors what they did the other half of the time. Whether this ratio would hold for other forces can't be said without further research.

Of the cases referred to detectives (either through receipt of an occurrence report or delivery of a suspect), 59 per cent are filed, 21 per cent are filed after a caution is given to the suspect, and 20 per cent result in a charge.[17] Not all occurrences have criminal elements to them and thus cannot be ''made'' into crimes. In other cases, it is not possible to produce a suspect, and the case must be filed away. The Peel detective makes one arrest every six shifts, and an average of two charges are laid against each accused.[18] In Metro Toronto in 1982, more than three charges were laid against each suspect.

What the detective wants and works for is a guilty plea, which produces four important benefits. First, the plea confirms that the police were right in laying charges. Second, it ensures that there will be no close scrutiny of police action by the court in this particular case, since the accused is agreeing to both a statement of fact and his own nefarious involvement. Third, the plea spares the detective the considerable work necessary for trial preparation. Last, the plea gives certainty in the courtroom — a matter of prime importance to the crown, the police and the accused.

The detective weighs two factors in deciding which occurrence to devote his attention to. He will first choose cases that have a good investigative lead, where there is a suspect or the trail is still warm. His second choice will be cases that have a good administrative payoff: cases that are serious or where public relations and senior officers demand some action be taken. Incidents involving a suspect in custody almost always receive first priority, since they can fulfil both criteria. As a rule of thumb, cases involving violence are high on the list, since usually there is a suspect associated with them. On the other hand, property crimes rarely yield a suspect at the outset, and thus are of lower priority. Yet the payoffs are reversed: crimes of violence usually produce a number of different stories and explanations, so it is relatively difficult to construct a case that the criminal justice system will determine is a crime, while in property offences the evidence (if found) is often conclusive enough to produce a strong case.

The patrol officer suggests the names of about half the suspects — either by arrest or by referring to them in the occurrence report. The detective turns up the other half by talking with the complainant or (more often) with informants who may have been involved to some extent in the incident.[19] Where a suspect can't be turned up or where the evidence seems unsatisfactory, the detective will usually convince the complainant that the case is not worth proceeding with and should be filed away.

A detective will go to great lengths to control a suspect once identified. The suspect will be put under informal arrest, perhaps by asking him or her to get into the police cruiser or to come down to the police station to talk. In both situations, the police want to put the suspect in a situation where his bargaining position is weakened and theirs is strengthened. If informal means fail, the suspect will be formally arrested and taken to the station where access to third parties — whether lawyers or friends — is regulated to the suspect's disadvantage.

The detective will then search the suspect's home. This search is not so much for the purpose of discovering evidence, but more to obtain information that will furnish levers for dealing with the suspect. Most homes contain material that is mildly embarrassing, or even incriminating: soft- or hard-core pornography, radical books, drugs, or telephone numbers of certain friends. Police use all such information against a suspect, making the search a most powerful tool. Detectives usually ask for the suspect's consent to the search (using strong psychological pressure by suggesting that reluctance to cooperate implies guilt).

If this doesn't work, a search warrant is obtained.

Finally, the detective asks the suspect to confess to some wrongdoing. Not only does a confession make a suspect feel guilty, but it also guarantees that a guilty plea will be obtained. For the detective, it hardly matters what the suspect pleads guilty to, since any plea justifies the arrest. Ericson found, as have other researchers, that two-thirds of all those arrested confess to an offence of some kind.[20]

Laying charges might be the most important work the detective does, since the charge is the asking price in plea bargaining.[21] Once in court, it is assumed that the suspect must be guilty of *something*, despite the official presumption of innocence until proven guilty. Detectives know from experience that nothing is lost by charging ''up'' — that is, laying a charge that may be more serious than the actual incident. Indeed, much is gained, since a guilty plea to a lower charge can always be accepted and the higher charge withdrawn, with few questions raised in the courtroom.

Usual practice is to lay two or more charges against a suspect for a single incident. Ericson notes five reasons for this.[22] First, more charges give greater leverage for a guilty plea and conviction. Second, further surveillance of the suspect both before and after trial is justified. Third, other occurrences can be cleared, improving the record of clearance by charge. (For instance, a break-and-enter suspect could find himself charged with offences from a great number of unsolved break and enters, even if evidence of his involvement is shaky.) Fourth, it becomes more difficult for a suspect to obtain bail: he is made more dependent on police, and more malleable. Finally, multiple charges make the suspect feel that he has done something wrong, that he is a criminal.

The climax of the detective's work is the plea-bargaining session. Negotiations with the defence lawyer are usually carried out by an overworked crown attorney, who must rely entirely on the notes and briefing provided by the detective. While detectives are formally silent during plea bargaining (and perhaps not even present), they are the controlling force. Ericson makes the following comments on the process:

> ...in plea bargaining it seems that everyone wins.
>
> The plea transactions were characterized by coercion, manipulation, and/or negotiation as the parties attempted to achieve the plea agreements they had in mind. Typically they each got something out of the agreements, resulting in the perception of a plea bargain. The detectives could ring up their credit charges and achieve the satisfaction of having their earlier decisions confirmed as the accused was convicted and made "criminal." The Crown Attorneys ensured that they obtained a conviction along with a predictable range of sentence. The lawyers could usually sell their clients on the idea that they achieved leniency in the form of a reasonable sentence and the withdrawal of some charges. In sum, they could each secure their own individual interests while giving the collective appearance that the accused had been given a fair deal.[23]

From a police point of view, the whole process culminating in a plea bargain is eminently successful. In the Ericson study, 96 per cent of those charged were convicted of something, and more than 80 per cent of cases were handled by a guilty plea.[24] Yet it should be noted that only one-fifth of cases referred to detectives are dealt with in this fashion: the remaining cases are resolved by being filed away as too difficult to solve or by giving the suspect a warning or other citation. In cases where a caution is given, and even in the rare instance where the court renders a not-guilty verdict, the detective has at least exerted a police presence that will convince the individual to tread more warily in the future.

The above description of day-to-day police work illustrates the distinction between the duties of the patrol officer and those of the detective, a division of responsibility that is borne out by the organization charts. However, a small number of large urban forces are now experimenting with team policing, blurring the differences. In this approach, a team of officers carries out all activities in a neighbourhood twenty-four hours a day. The team includes patrol officers, detectives and a specialized staff, such as youth officers. Duties are shared among members of the team. An officer does not turn a suspect over to a detective for processing, but instead sees the case through to finality, including plea bargaining.

Advocates of team policing argue that breaking down divisions between patrol officers and detectives, between generalists and specialists, improves the force's morale and individuals' sense of job satisfaction. Greater efficiencies in handling minor and frequent crime are said to result, and thanks to the team's more intimate knowledge of the community, better community relations emerge.

Police Specialization

In addition to the general services provided by the patrol officer and the detective, police forces also undertake more specific services. However, these have traditionally been regarded as being best provided by officers with basic, non-specialized skills. This attitude is reflected in hiring and promotional practices, where no premium is placed on special talents, as we shall see.

Some specific services do require highly developed skills, such as in accounting, office management, communications and computers. These positions are filled by "civilian" staff who are not considered suitable to be formally part of the police force, although they work for the organization. In practice, however, there is often little difference between civilians' and officers' jobs.

The idea of "civilianization" as a method of increasing specialized skills in police organizations is becoming more common. Some forces, recognizing their limited management skills, have hired civilian chief administrative officers, thus permitting significant civilian power in police decisions. One force has hired a civilian as deputy chief. On the other hand, the 1982 Hickling/Johnston report on management of the Metro Toronto Police recommended that the generalist role of the officer be emphasized even more.

The generalist bias — still the dominant view — is evident when the few examples of specialization are studied closely. The most widely known example of police specialization is the youth squad. Virtually every force has one, and this particular example of moving away from a generalist approach is widely accepted. The Ottawa youth squad is a typical one.

The Ottawa Youth Liaison Section was formed in 1964, recognizing that "police agencies should expand their role in the area of juvenile crime prevention and rehabilitation."[25] The police wanted a "consistent and purposeful" response and saw this section as providing it. Five goals were established:

● to coordinate the force's activities in relation to youth;

- to set up a system that would allow for study and analysis of delinquency;
- to get into the network of social agencies;
- to respond appropriately — laying charges or giving warnings once the juvenile has been contacted; and
- to establish appropriate response to juvenile delinquency problems.

Lifting this function out of the matrix of the other police functions was not easy, and the authors (see note 25 above) go to considerable pains to explain that YLS officers are still part of the force. For instance:

> Although the YLS was established as a separate section, it operates under the same philosophical principles as other sections of the force. A youth officer remains a policeman and must view his primary role as protection of society and perceive that all individuals, regardless of age, be held accountable for their actions....A police officer transferred to the YLS does not become any less a police officer with regard to this goal.[26]

Officers must meet three criteria to join the YLS: an interest in juvenile relations; "the ability to interact socially without becoming frustrated"; and five years' experience on the force. The reasons given for the last qualification say much about attitudes to specialization:

> One [reason for the experience requirement] is to allow for the development of all facets of police work in the individual: the Ottawa Police Force perceives its police officers as "generalists" and to transfer an individual into a more specialized area without that individual having experienced general police duties would be

detrimental to that officer and to the force overall.
Secondly, to maintain the crucial rapport with the
uniformed section, it is necessary that the youth officers be respected, and this can be more easily achieved
if members of the uniform section and youth section
have known each other personally through working
together over a period of time.[27]

After selection by the YLS, officers attend police school
to be trained for their new duties.

The YLS is divided into several subsections: school
patrols; safety films and lectures; court liaison; records
and analysis; crime prevention programs; and processing juveniles whom the section makes contact with.
Investigation is left to regular police channels: "It is
felt that the youth officer can communicate and deal
with the juvenile more effectively and openly if he is
not viewed as the investigating officer." Strong links
are maintained with a network of social agencies, and
while the YLS recognizes its role as a police agency,
it sees itself as part of the youth-serving community.

One of the most important tools for the YLS is the
exercise of discretion. Guidelines have been established, and they make it clear that the job is not only
one of pressing for a conviction:

Where a juvenile is accused of an offence and the
facts and circumstances are sufficient to substantiate
a charge, the youth officer has a choice of two courses
of action. These are: charging the juvenile with the
offence and proceeding through the juvenile court; or
deferring action, not exercising legal proceedings and
relying on the youth officer, the guardians and/or a
social agency to handle the problem. To assist the
youth officer in determining whether a juvenile should
be charged with an offence, the Ottawa Police Force

has established several guidelines to be considered at the time of the decision. These guidelines are not seen as rules to be rigidly followed, but rather as general working principles.[28]

The guidelines indicate that charges should be pursued in cases involving physical violence and injury, serious property damage, weapons or multiple offences. This is one of the few times that a police force states, in black and white, that in some cases charges should not be laid even though an offence has clearly been committed. The YLS has gone further yet, setting up a program in 1976 to divert juveniles from the court system. The YLS sees its role as a social one, as opposed to the headlong prosecution of individuals through the criminal justice system.

Most other large forces in Canada have a youth squad which shares the concerns and values of the Ottawa Youth Liaison Section. Although the other forces may not be as explicit about the diversionary role of the officers or the structuring of how discretion should be exercised, their behaviour is similar. Apparently the nature of specialization in police work leads to a clear enunciation of goals, and an attempt to structure the exercise of discretion, two of the more significant "grey" areas of policing.

A growing field of specialization is policing the family. Police fear the domestic call, since it involves entering a residence where space is much better known to the disputants than to the officer, and the disputants have much in common. Emotional energies, often fueled by alcohol, are high, and weapons are as close as the knives in the kitchen drawer. Children are in the bedroom next door. At the best of times a domestic dispute is depressing: at the worst it is rife with danger.

As well, domestic disputes seem to break out in the same households again and again. Some couples are well known to the police, since they squabble every few weeks. Others might fight but not come to the attention of the police until the seventh or eighth occurrence. The domestic response team is the special squad set up to deal with these situations.

The first such Canadian squad was created in London, Ontario. There, officers began by referring domestic disputes to social workers, but this experiment had a number of shortcomings. The safety of the social worker was not guaranteed, and the referral arrangement did nothing to reduce the apparent antagonism between the police and social agencies.

A variant of the London model was tried in Toronto. A domestic response team would consist of a social worker and a police officer working together. Social workers were chosen on the basis of their experience in crisis intervention and their knowledge of minority languages and cultures. Officers were chosen from the community relations division on the basis of interest in, and commitment to, this undertaking, ability to work with civilians, and willingness to forgo promotional opportunities. (This last criterion was inserted to ensure that officers would not drop out before the first year of the experiment was concluded — yet one might infer that this is another example of bias against specialists in the force.)

The training, which was equally shared by the social agencies and by the police, explored the expected areas of crisis intervention, law and social resources. The peak work times for the team were weekends and evenings, particularly that outlet for the week's frustrations, Saturday night.

Teams would be called in whenever an officer

thought they might be of some use. This was the problem. For some officers, a domestic crisis was resolved the minute the couple stopped yelling at each other, while others recognized that as the moment the team should be called in. Some officers feared that a call to a team was an admission of failure. Thus, the team was utterly dependent on the cooperation and understanding of the rest of the force.[29]

The domestic response team is a good example of how police can change modes of operation, including collaborating successfully with non-police personnel, to work on a special social problem. Examples like this should dissolve any concern that police must be set apart from other community agencies or government functions, lest the force's integrity be eroded.

A third example of specialization is the policing of labour. Traditionally, police have been opposed to organized labour, and there are countless examples of police breaking strikes by disrupting picket lines and protecting management interests. The RCMP has a history of being used as strikebreakers, as do most other large forces.

Yet new directions are being considered. The Hamilton-Wentworth Police Department formed a labour squad in the early 1970s to deal with the labour conflicts in this highly industrialized and highly unionized area. While the squad consists of only two officers, its effect has been enormous. Its main goal has been the reduction of incidents and arrests on picket lines — and to use 1982 as an example, although the region experienced eighteen strikes involving 6,000 workers and only twenty-eight strike-free days, there were no arrests on the strike line.

The officers involved make a point of talking to both management and labour in a dispute, finding out what each expects, and indicating that while the officers could not become middlemen, they could guarantee that each side is treated fairly in their own terms. Companies are assured that vehicles carrying materials or personnel necessary for the maintenance of the plant would get through the picket line; the unions are assured that police would not aid company vehicles or personnel for the purpose of breaking the strike. Union members would be warned when authorized vehicles could be expected, and after demonstrations of a set period, say ten minutes, such vehicles would be permitted through the line.

The labour squad acts as a body whose function is to keep the peace, and it makes appropriate agreements to ensure that result. Some might argue that the letter of the law — which says any person or vehicle is entitled to go through the line — is not upheld. Yet the past has shown strict enforcement could result in violence and property damage, and might raise emotions to a level where chances of a settlement decline.

The three examples noted above all involve a rethinking of how policing might be carried out. These kinds of specialization are distinct from those areas where traditional policing has been simply intensified, such as detectives assigned to homicide or fraud or morality bureaus. In those instances, it is not unusual expertise that is required, but a honing of general patrol and detective skills. The examples of specialization noted here involve a comprehensive look at the service provided, and result in a clear definition of goals and objectives, a structuring of discretion, and a new relationship with other organizations in the social order.

Two other kinds of police specialization must be

touched on. One is the arrangement used to respond to organized crime. As discussed in chapter 2, the crime corporation is such a pervasive animal that traditional crime-control methods have proven unsuccessful in taming it, and police authorities have had to devise new approaches.

It seems generally agreed that effective action starts with the appointment of a team of officers who are given almost unlimited time to gather information. The team must have a distinct identity, with members appointed on a full-time basis so that their investigative energies are not siphoned off by other cases. As with the Criminal Law Enforcement Unit in Vancouver, the team often includes lawyers, and its function is to prosecute as well as investigate. Given the difficulty in tying down the relationships between various people, which is such an integral part of organized crime work, no distinction is made between the gathering of information and the use that will be made of it in court — lawyers are involved at every stage to ensure that no case will be thrown out on technicalities.

The process is not inexpensive, and it is very time-consuming — particularly if the accused provokes a repetition of trials, as in the Volpe case. Here again the benefits of police specialization are evident. Goals come into focus, discretion is structured, and relations with non-police personnel are increased.

The other kind of specialization that deserves mention is police political intelligence, or the secret service. This issue has been subjected to substantial debate at the federal level, resulting in the establishment of an organization separate from the RCMP to deal with policing of national security matters. The McDonald Commission report that preceded the creation of the new Security Service mentions many of the problems surrounding specific intelligence operations, and one case deserves mention.

Praxis was a Toronto group interested in social change at the city level. During the 1960s it helped secure community organizers for the poor and provided advice to other activist groups. A paper prepared by the Security Service identified Praxis, along with other groups which espoused a New Left philosophy, as a threat to society. The Security Service feared that this "EPO" — Extra Parliamentary Opposition — would destroy the parliamentary system. The McDonald Commission commented on this report as follows:

> As with other papers we have reviewed in writing this chapter, the EPO paper demonstrates an insensitivity to the difference between a threat to Canada's security on the one hand and legitimate dissent on the other. The careless use of language to create sinister impressions was one manifestation of this insensitivity. Thus certain individuals, when they joined or attempted to influence an organization, were said to be "penetrating" it....
>
> The aspect of the EPO matter which we find especially objectionable, however, was the circulation outside of the Security Service of a paper which names particular individuals and records many of their thoughts without any reference to their planning or engaging in activity relating to terrorism or serious political violence. Thus the paper was a prime example of the dangers which a security intelligence system can pose to two cherished values in our society — the right of association and the right to privacy.[30]

These are the two key issues raised by the gathering of political intelligence by the police. They attract no easy solutions. The removal of the Security Service from the RCMP to a separate agency does not alleviate the problem: it just reduces the opportunity for the RCMP to use the information it has gathered in unto-ward ways (although there is nothing to stop the new organization from doing that).

This function involved some specialization within the RCMP, but given its shadowy nature, it is unclear the degree to which goals and objectives were clarified or how discretion was structured. Certainly relations with non-police personnel were no better than they were in other police activities. Thus, it is difficult to conclude that the benefits of specialization apply to the secret service branch. Specialization was probably a function of the secrecy with which this work was carried out.

At the local level, police also serve an intelligence function, defined by the Toronto force as monitoring organized crime and reporting major crime activities. Information is not available about the extent to which urban police gather information of a political and social nature. On a city level, the degree of specialization for this function appears limited and no more extensive than that of other detective units.

Recruitment

Unlike virtually every other organization in the modern industrial state, police forces allow new staff to enter only at the bottom. No matter what his experience or training, a would-be police officer must start at the same place as everybody else, the bottom, although officers being transferred from other forces are often permitted to enter the organization somewhere up the line. Thus, recruitment policies as well as the under-lying assumptions about basic skill levels are of great importance to policing authorities.

All police forces have minimum requirements for

recruits. Once these are met, a lengthy, complex process unfolds as the force decides on a particular applicant. Because of the high social status of police officers and the handsome remuneration they receive, the number of hopefuls always exceeds the number of available positions, giving authorities a large pool of applicants to draw on.

Minimum requirements vary from force to force. Most forces insist on Canadian citizenship, or that the applicant is a British subject. In an attempt to attract officers from among new arrivals from other countries before they settle into some other line of work, Calgary accepts those with landed-immigrant status.

Age restrictions vary. Ottawa and Vancouver accept candidates between 18 and 35; Regina between 19 and 31. Calgary has a lower limit of 19 but no ceiling; Toronto has a lower limit of 21 but, like many other forces, takes on younger people as cadets until they are 21 years old, when they can enter the regular stream. Some 60 per cent of recruits in Toronto have served the force as cadets.

Forces have different attitudes to height and weight requirements. Ottawa, Vancouver and Regina agree that females must be at least 5 feet 4 inches, but they differ about males. Vancouver has a minimum of 5 feet 8 inches, a standard adopted by Regina only in 1982 (Regina has a maximum height of 6 feet 4 inches), and Ottawa has a minimum of 5 feet 10 inches. Calgary simply requires that weight be commensurate with height. Regina is alone in demanding that male weight be between 150 and 220 pounds, with a 118 minimum for females. There is no clear consensus about the body size of a good police recruit.

Ottawa requires recruits to have ''unaided perfect vision,'' but most other forces permit imperfect vision within limits if it can be corrected by glasses or lenses. Calgary has set requirements about degrees of red and green colour blindness. All forces dictate that recruits must be physically fit and in good health; Calgary suggests "average or better physical condition."

Educational requirements are virtually the same across the country: grade 12 or its equivalent. Higher educational attainment is measured later in the recruitment process through written and oral tests. Applicants to any force must have a valid driver's licence.

Any set of entry requirements are bound to reflect certain assumptions about the nature of the job. In the case of police work, it appears that many forces assume that certain physical characteristics are of primary importance and that no matter what kinds of specialized skills one might have, they count for naught if physical standards are not met. In a study for the Metro Toronto Police Commission on related questions, John Clement succinctly summed up what seem to be widely shared assumptions about physical standards: "The strenuous nature of the work, the desirability of commanding an aura of competence and authority, physical superiority, psychological advantage, visibility and appearance, etc., cannot be disregarded."[31] One might question whether indeed that is the nature of police work, and if so, which physical characteristics impart the desired impressions.

In assessing height and weight standards, Clement concluded that hard and fast standards might discriminate against minorities. He found too that for this reason many American forces had abandoned such standards. Other forces watered down requirements so far that they became almost meaningless. Los Angeles, for instance, says any male over 5 feet 6 inches can join the force; those who don't make that standard can try Chicago, where the minimum is two inches lower. Clement recommended that height should simply be proportionate to weight, as in Calgary.

In Toronto, candidates who have made it through the screening process are next subjected to a series of physical and mental tests, and intensive personal scrutiny by examining officers. This second process again contains its own assumptions. It is not unfair to say that in the absence of any contrary directive, any organization can be expected to take on people much like those who are already employed. A police force that has encouraged minority recruitment in the past can be expected to continue to do so. A force that prides itself on physical size and stamina will hire big, tough men. Supporting this bias is a comparable assumption on the part of the applicant: he would not apply to a force unless he felt that he would fit in. Like attracts like, and the two reinforce each other.

Accordingly, the post-entry phase of recruitment is the critical one in determining who will become a police officer. After reviewing Toronto's entry requirements, Clement suggested that a much fuller study of recruitment practices be undertaken. The firm of Hickling/Johnston, Management Consultants, was retained for this purpose. Their study recommended a Weighted Selections Standards System closely paralleling the RCMP's system. The Hickling/Johnston recommendations were adopted by the Toronto Police Commission in 1980, and since this system is considered state of the art for determining who should uphold law and order in Canada, it is worth reviewing in some detail.

There are six steps in the system prior to the final decision about an applicant. The first step is the basic pre-screen, discussed above.

Step two introduces a set of assessments of the applicant. The applicant is rated in five areas, with points given in each. The maximum number of points is 300. One must amass at least 190 points to move on to step three. The five factors are as follows:

- *Age* (maximum 75 points): The optimum age is between 23 and 25. The score falls off by 5 points a year outside this range. Applicants older than 35 receive a zero score. The Hickling/Johnston report notes: "Candidates older than the mid-20's tend to begin to adopt lifestyle and work habits that diverge from the requirements of a police career."[32]
- *Height* (maximum 75 points): The ideal height for a male is between 5 feet 9 inches and 6 feet 3 inches, for a female between 5 feet 3½ inches and 6 feet 3 inches. Since average heights on a national basis correspond with the lower range for both sexes, it is thought that 45 per cent of the population will receive maximum points here. The rationale for the recommended heights is set out in the report:

  > Research studies conducted during the 1970's identified such height/performance factors as: a minimum height required to see better in crowds when helping to control public disorders; larger stature required for drivers and pedestrians to better see the officer directing traffic; difficulties of shorter constables receiving peer acceptance and hence inhibiting necessary team work; and smaller officers attracting a greater incidence of citizen attacks. Rigorous scientific research studies have, however, failed to establish a conclusive correlation between police performance and height.[33]

The report notes that "research studies have discovered evidence of declining police officer effectiveness at heights exceeding approximately 6 feet 3 inches caused primarily by deteriorating physical condition (for example, back disorders — with resulting higher absenteeism)."[34]

- *Education* (maximum 75 points): A university degree gets maximum points. A community college diploma rates 60 points, an approved law enforcement or criminal justice diploma 65. A grade 12 diploma is worth 45 points. In this system, it is better to be tall and somewhat educated than short and well educated.

- *Previous work experience* (maximum 50 points): Maximum points are awarded to an applicant with three or more years related work experience showing a pattern of increasing work responsibilities. The Hickling/Johnston study provides a list of jobs that, somehow, are considered related: door-to-door salesman, real estate agent, athletic coach, bartender, Canadian Armed Forces, and group leader, to name a few. Jobs thought to be unrelated to the world of law enforcement include chef, accountant, librarian, office worker and technical service man.[35]

- *Demonstrated community involvement* (maximum 25 points): A list of appropriate community groups are set out, including associations of all kinds and volunteer organizations.[36] Lower scores are awarded for the applicant who is simply a member rather than a leader. A complete lack of community involvement results in rejection.

Provided the score on step two is satisfactory, the applicant moves on. Step three is the skills work profile, involving four different measures, with a maximum rating of 300 points. The minimum is 175. The measures are:

- *Intelligence* (maximum 100 points): This measure involves general and verbal aptitude tests, designed so that 10 per cent of the population would receive maximum points.
- *Written communication* (maximum 100 points): Applicants must write two essays, each taking fifteen minutes. Judgment is made on the basis of relevance, maturity and communication.
- *Physical capability* (maximum 100 points): Specific points are given for various exercises (for men, 36 push-ups are required for maximum points in that category, 22 for women), and a measure of body fat is taken.
- *Psychological testing*: A test is administered during this step, but not scored until step four.

Step four is the Recruiting Officer's Assessment. It consists of a ninety-minute interview followed by a short spelling test. The officer appraises the applicant in terms of appearance, ability to perform in pressure situations, common sense and good judgment, integrity and honesty, sensitivity, maturity, dependability and reliability, cooperation, public service orientation, and so forth. It is a thorough job interview. The maximum attainable is 600, with 50 points allocated to the spelling test, which gives the recruiting officer a chance to see the applicant under pressure for a short period of time.

Step five reviews capability deficiencies. The psychological test is reviewed, and the applicant is rejected if minimum levels are not achieved. A medical examination is conducted as well as a security check. If there are no negative signs, the applicant proceeds to the final step.

Step six consists of a background assessment of five different factors, with a maximum of 300 points:

- *Residence check* (maximum 100 points): The applicant's residence is visited, and interviews are conducted with parents, spouse, landlord and neighbours.
- *Reference interview* (maximum 100 points): Two former employers or personal references are interviewed in person.
- *Reference check* (no points awarded): A further reference is interviewed by telephone.
- *Written inquiries* (no points awarded) are made to verify information provided by the applicant.
- *A credit check* (no points awarded) is made.

On the basis of these five factors, the recruiting officer assigns a rating within a further discretionary 100 points, thus completing step six.

Points are now totalled. Of the 1,500 points possible, the applicant must score at least 980 to be accepted. If there are more acceptable candidates than positions, the top scorers are the first hired.

Critics of the Weighted Selections Standards System note that while the system is sophisticated — or at least complicated — it only hires individuals who fit within a given set of criteria. Distinctions about the specific job to be done are not built into this system; instead the assumption is that police officers are generalists, all doing the same sort of job, requiring the same levels of skills and specialization.

Criticisms of Recruitment Practices

One of the pressures that provoked the Hickling/Johnston study on selection standards was the complaint that the membership of the Toronto police force, and others across the country, was not fairly representative of visible minorities. But will changing entry requirements relieve this problem in any appreciable way? Many sociologists agree that a common characteristic of organizations is to shun the different, to arrange the organization's affairs — however unconsciously — to protect those already inside. Thus, the minority problem might be systemic, and opening the entry gate may not result in any staffing change within the organization.

A recent study suggests six reasons why minorities do not respond to recruitment appeals:[37]

- They do not view police work as an attractive career because they tend to perceive police organizations as predominantly white. They wouldn't feel at home.
- There are few role models for minorities in police forces, particularly at the senior levels. For them, law enforcement appears to be another dead-end job where career development is limited.
- Joining a police force is tantamount to "selling out" or "joining the enemy" in the eyes of one's peers.
- For better-qualified minority individuals, other careers will be financially and socially more rewarding.
- Many individuals from minority groups seriously doubt they are wanted in a police force. At best they would be tolerated, but not accepted.
- Individuals feel that they will never be accepted as law enforcement officials by a predominantly white public.

Overcoming these kinds of problems would require more than an improved selection system. Numerous forces have devised outreach programs where minorities are encouraged to make a career of police work. Other forces are attempting to fast-track minority officers to senior positions so that at least some of the assumptions made by those outside the force about career blockage are blunted. Unfortunately, these initiatives are sometimes wrecked on the shoals of racial bias, such as when in 1980 Cardinal Carter told the Toronto police chief to instruct his officers that they should not call black officers ''niggers,'' even in jest. No minority program has a ghost of a chance to succeed in such an environment.

A second pressure leading to the new Weighted Selection Standards System was the sentiment that officers did not meet high enough educational standards. A 1980 Toronto study found that 45 per cent of senior officers on the Metro Toronto force had grade 10 education or less, reflecting the minimum standards in effect when the officers joined the force some years ago. Only one senior officer had a bachelor of arts degree.[38]

The public wanted more college graduates on the force. Canadian law professor and former policeman Alan Grant argued that forces should be required to reach a quota of university-educated officers, on penalty of reduced provincial grants.[39] Others suggested that appointments to senior positions should only be open to officers who had at least some university training, if not a degree. Given the fear most organizations have of bright new talent (and the upsets that the new talent will bring), police forces could feel threatened by this kind of approach.

There are disagreements about the wisdom of requir-

ing higher educational achievements. American criminologist Herman Goldstein notes that it has never been
proven that university graduates are more tolerant or
sensitive in their contacts with citizens, although graduates do appear to be less authoritarian than others,
perhaps having achieved added social skills.[40] More
to the point, by hiring university graduates, a police
force will begin to better represent a cross section of
society, as well as include — for what it is worth —
some of its more educated members.

Goldstein believes that highly educated officers could
easily become frustrated in their jobs, grow cynical
and look for ways out:

> If a different sort of person is to be attracted into the
> police service, change must occur not only in recruit-
> ment, selection and training programmes, but in the
> organizational environment as well. Otherwise, new
> personnel will have little chance of surviving in the
> organization. The pressures for conformity are so strong
> that a new officer will either be forced into the police
> subculture, with the values and orientation of the larger
> group replacing his own, or his life will be made so
> unpleasant he will decide to resign.[41]

Police reaction to the debate has been to put much
greater emphasis on training officers currently
employed: to educate the recruited rather than recruiting the educated. While this approach certainly results
in improved educational levels, it does not produce
the other benefits that come with hiring persons who
already meet these higher standards.

Training

Once an applicant successfully completes the selection
process and is hired by a police force, he or she becomes

a recruit and begins formal training. Educational programs are run by provincial authorities (and in the case of larger centres like Montreal and Toronto, by the police forces themselves) at special police schools. There are a number of these schools in Canada: the Atlantic Police Academy in Prince Edward Island; the Canadian Police College in Ottawa; the Aylmer Police College, run by the Ontario Provincial Police; the Saskatchewan Police College; and the British Columbia Police Academy. As well, the RCMP runs several training academies.

Police training is not part of a general educational experience such as one finds in nursing, engineering, dentistry and law; nor is it integrated with technical programs at a community college. Instead, police academies are set apart from other educational institutions. For instance, the Aylmer Police College is located in a small town south of London, Ontario. The college is the main industry in town. Recruits will not be sullied by students who are pursuing different lines of thought or different social directions.

Training at a police academy lasts for three or four months. The recruit is expected to board there, usually in a dormitory, for this period. Training touches both philosophical questions of policing and criminal justice, and practical matters. The subjects taught at the Saskatchewan Police College during 1981 are representative:

- *Larger issues*: Criminal law; psychology and police; image and ethics; psychology; officer/violator relationships; prevention of crime; police/Native relations.
- *Working tools of the trade*:
    — Patrol, tactics and techniques; emergency

response; contacting suspicious persons on the beat; responding to complaints; domestic complaints.

— Principles of investigation; investigation of burglary, fire and arson; juvenile investigation; bombs and explosives; child molesters; missing runaway juveniles.

— Identifying suspects; obtaining physical descriptions; witness perceptions.

— Homicide; drugs; rape crisis; sex offences; fraud and related subjects; motor vehicle thefts; accidents and traffic control; liquor; gun control.

— Summary offences; first aid; crime scene to courtroom; communications.

- *Personal skill development*: Effective presentations; discipline and deportment; observation and memory; report writing; defensive driving; pursuit driving; firearm training; Canadian Police Information Services; testifying in court; use of notebook; lifesaving; swimming.
- *Social concerns*: Alcoholism; communication with the deaf; dealing with the handicapped; Native treaties history.

Courses offered by the other academies show some changes from this curriculum. For instance, the Aylmer course replaces a session on Native treaties with one on multiculturalism.[42]

There are two overriding influences imparted by this training, neither of which relates to the subject matter taught. First, as already noted, this learning experience is isolated from that of other students preparing themselves for employment. It is fair to say that from the earliest days of training, police officers are set apart, as though they are being told that they are different from everyone else.

Second, depersonalization is a significant aspect of training. Not only are recruits separated from family and friends for several months, but every day they are subject to drills where they must line up and respond to orders. This training helps ensure that the recruit loses his sense of individuality, at least enough to fit within the police system.

Suggestions are often made that the curriculum should be expanded to cover contemporary issues: relations with minorities, policing demonstrations, the law and women, and so forth. In many cases, these subjects *are* incorporated into courses, and specialists are brought in to teach and lead discussion for half a day or more. Yet in an environment where recruits are learning to think of themselves as an exclusive, depersonalized group rather than to empathize with marginalized groups in society, the degree to which these issues are absorbed will not be extensive.

Three other criticisms should be noted. Anyone who has attended university will find the police college curriculum unchallenging. As well, the training program makes certain exclusionary assumptions about who recruits are — persons who are willing to be separated from families and friends to live in dormitories, persons whose skills levels are relatively low. A recruit who is not willing to subject himself to this training period will not be permitted to become a police officer. Last, the curriculum does not touch on such questions as discretion, police deviance and its control, corruption, or police governance. These are all meaty questions affecting the everyday work of the officer; yet they are not addressed.

The selection system is geared to ensure that most recruits will successfully complete the training period, thus not putting at risk what is clearly a considerable expense. Recruits who will be working for larger forces go on to further training courses within the forces for a month or two.

At the conclusion of the course, or courses, graduation ceremonies are held, and the recruit is accepted into the force that originally hired him. Preliminary training is complete.

Retraining

Police forces appear to make much greater use of employee training programs than do other employers. Officers are expected to participate in weekly in-house activities and are encouraged to take advantage of more extensive programs run by both policing authorities and by outside agencies.

The most common form of police retraining is a weekly briefing session, usually held on the least busy time for the force, Sunday morning. Officers are filled in on changes to the laws they must enforce, and there is usually discussion about current social problems. All officers must attend at least once a month. These sessions permit officers to brush up on issues that might come up during a normal day on the beat.

The following summarizes a Sunday-morning program run by the Hamilton-Wentworth regional force in mid-1981:[43]

- Discussion of a new amendment to the Criminal Code dealing with criminal rates of interest.
- Discussion of the Environmental Protection Act of Ontario, especially applications relevant to an offi-

cer on patrol, for example, burning garbage in a backyard or littering.

- Discussion of a number of common problematic occurrences. For example: Officers are called to a tavern and told a customer will not pay his bar bill of $25. The customer admits he rang up the bill but does not intend to pay. What does the officer do? (Answer: The officer can't do much of anything. Section 322[1] of the Criminal Code states that a criminal offence occurs when food or lodging is obtained fraudulently, but it does not cover liquor. The bartender will have to pursue a civil remedy.)
- Acting out an event involving people in conflict, and discussing what the best police response might be. One example dealt with a fight between a landlord and a tenant; a second was a family dispute involving possible mental illness; a third was an attempt to provoke a racial reaction from an officer.

Sunday-morning sessions such as these are straightforward, dealing with nuts-and-bolts issues.

Many larger forces augment these sessions with refresher courses, and police academies offer similar courses to all officers. The Hamilton force, for instance, runs a three-week course that officers must take every four years. The 1980 course had a curriculum of standard fare: police powers of search, force and arrests; traffic laws; fraud; weapons; personal skills such as report writing and transactional analysis; crisis intervention; emergencies and first aid; police and multiculturalism.

A second, more extensive, kind of training is offered in two streams by police colleges across Canada. There are specialized courses that cover subjects such as: criminal investigation; identification; colour photography; fraud investigation; forensic accounting; youth officer duties; traffic law and collision investigation; organized crime and crime intelligence; traffic supervision. The second stream is for officers who hope to move up the police hierarchy. These courses concentrate on management skills at junior, intermediate and senior levels.

Further, most forces offer to pay for a sizable chunk of the costs of approved courses at a university or other post-secondary institution. Yet the courses available lack the same element as those run by policing agencies themselves: they do not offer critical analysis of how policing works or discuss what options are available in pursuing a safe and ordered society.

Police Management

Responsibility for officers and detectives, recruitment and training, and all other police policy, is in the hands of police management. Management can provide stability and continuity or effect change.

At the top of the organizational pyramid is the police chief. Because of the way that police officers are recruited, a chief has usually been a cop for all of his working life. He tends to be undereducated in the formal sense, experienced in a narrow slice of society, and has little management expertise. Most police training is for the production of followers rather than leaders, and those who manage to obtain leadership positions do so because of their ability to maintain police practices and traditions.

Several authors express disparaging views about the typical police chief. One American chief states that "most chiefs are grateful that they have at last made it to the top" and they "don't see the job as a challenge; they see it as a sinecure. They've made it to the top and they are not going to jeopardize their position by setting new goals and moving ahead.''[44] A Pennsylvania study seems to confirm these observations, finding that police executives are much more submissive to authority than the general population and that they ''appear to have a greater lack of insight into their own limitations than the general population and greater social conformist tendencies than the population as a whole.''[45] Thus, it is not realistic to expect that a new chief will, say, push for modernization in management techniques or changes in the police bureaucracy that will make it more participatory in nature.

Some forces have attempted to break the cycle that produces chiefs who are loath to innovate. Many Western Canadian cities require that a candidate for chief has worked for another police force so that there is at least some broadening of horizons. Many forces, however, don't even attempt to attract outside applicants. Some critics have suggested basic university training as a prerequisite for the top position in the force.

Police departments invariably use the most rudimentary of management systems — rule by regulation. Procedures are specified in great detail, supposedly covering everything that is permissible and what is not, as well as setting out what will happen if a regulation is transgressed. It is difficult to think of any other bureaucracy that is run in such a way — outside, perhaps, of the military at war.

The regulations of the Metro Toronto Police, about 100 pages long and approved by the Toronto Police Commission, are typical of those for large forces. The public is familiar with Regulation 4.31.16, controlling the length of hair:

A male member of the force, while in uniform, will ensure that his hair, sideburns and moustache are kept neat, clean and well trimmed, and particularly that:
— hair showing at the back of the head below which a uniform cap is worn, shall be no longer than one inch and shall taper towards the edges and downwards towards the centre of the neck to no closer than one half inch above the collar. The remainder of the neck shall be clean shaven.

The regulations go on for some paragraphs on the subject of sideburns, moustaches and women's hairstyles, noting that "ringlets, ponytails and afro style hair will not be worn while in uniform."

This set of rules is rigorously followed. In February, 1981, an officer was charged with insubordination for not trimming his moustache as ordered. The officer felt his moustache was consistent with its length of the last several years and that other officers had similar moustaches. Subsequent to his charge, the officer was required to work on a beat for ten days, then at the Police College for three months. The officer appealed the case to the Ontario Police Commission, the ultimate arbiter in Ontario for disciplinary matters.

By majority decision, the police commission rejected the officer's appeal. In speaking for the majority, Commissioner John MacBeth stated:

From one point of view this matter arose over a quarter inch or so of moustache. To many this appears to be a trivial matter which has caused problems out of all proportion to the subject matter involved. However, when it comes to appearance a quarter of an inch does make a marked difference and it was by this amount that the regulations were eventually altered. Constable Murphy certainly did not regard the difference as trivial. More to the point, the matter at issue is not the length of the moustache but the refusal to obey a direct order.[46]

The regulations provide an effective management tool to require compliance with orders. They serve other functions such as outlining various rules of the road. Regulations describe police rankings, when to salute, various kinds of police awards, the confidentiality of various kinds of information, the use of firearms and the reporting thereon, and promotions. The regulations are also very precise about the most common of actions, such as using the telephone. Regulation 5.7.3 states: "Members shall not leave a caller waiting on 'hold' for a period of time without frequent assurance to the caller that his call is being attended to. When possible, a member shall obtain the name and telephone number of the caller and return the call if there is likely to be prolonged delay in assisting."

While this rule is not unreasonable, the fact that it is written down says much about the relationship between employer and employee. Most employees would be insulted to have this procedure spelled out to them in writing. Yet police regulations are rife with similar examples, from being required to report when radio equipment is not working properly (Reg. 4.19.1), to being courteous to other members of the force (Reg. 4.23.1), to not talking with someone so much that they don't perform their job well (Reg. 4.32.1). Such over-regulation is suffocating.

Many regulations have no relationship to the kinds of activities engaged in by officers in the latter half of the twentieth century. One series of regulations (3.13) defines the job of an officer in terms of being posted to a specific beat where the officer will stand on guard, a once-important activity that is now rarely seen except as punishment.

As Commissioner MacBeth notes, the regulations are there to be enforced. Management flows from them. Charges can be laid, and a disciplinary hearing conducted, leading to reprimands and punishment.

It should be noted, however, that in some cases, regulations can be interpreted by management in a very relaxed fashion. Take Regulation 4.28.5, dealing with the important matter of soliciting:

> No member shall, at any time, for his own benefit or that of another person solicit or accept, either directly or indirectly, any gift, token, benefit or discount, when such gift, benefit or discount could reasonably be considered to be offered:
>
> — in return for past, present or anticipated service;
> — in return for the withholding or omission of any past, present or anticipated service;
> — only to members of the force by reason of their membership therein.

Members of the Metro Toronto police force are regularly offered discounts by firms advertising in the force's monthly magazine, *News and Views*. The Metro Toronto Police Commission has ruled that the regulation is not infringed by such offers, since the benefits do not apply just to members of the force — they are available to *retired* officers too! This interpretation shows the extent to which the regulations are a discretionary management tool that can be used by senior officers to permit some ''grey'' activities while suppressing other behaviour felt improper.

Police Unionism

Rank-and-file employees have responded to this oppressive management strategy by forming police associations and, where permitted, unions. All cities have some form of police association or union, and bargaining takes place in a collective fashion no matter what form the organization takes. In Newfoundland, Quebec, Ontario and Alberta, legislation prohibits police to be members of unions; yet the strong police associations in those provinces differ little from the formal unions allowed elsewhere except for a legislated right to strike.

Police strikes are legal, although rare, in New Brunswick, Nova Scotia, Manitoba, Saskatchewan and British Columbia.[47] Elsewhere, disputes are resolved by binding arbitration, a process that is much resented by organizations that prefer to negotiate a settlement rather than seeing management hide behind arbitration when negotiations get tough. Frustrations with binding arbitration can lead to illegal walkouts. In 1969 the Police Brotherhood in Montreal staged a spectacular illegal strike to support its membership's demands. Within a few hours of the withdrawal of police services and after Montreal police literally kidnapped Quebec Provincial Police sent in to maintain order, the city disintegrated into lawlessness and the Brotherhood was given the financial package that had been denied in arbitration.[48] The total removal of police presence resulted in a social collapse, providing an excellent example of the symbolic nature of police in society — their function as a cohesive force.

These employee protection groups appear stronger than most other employee organizations. While benefits bargained for include financial matters, they often touch on questions about how the police force operates. In Montreal, when the police commission rejected the idea of a four-day work week, the Brotherhood simply implemented it on its own, and it is now a reality in that city. In Toronto, the Police Association bargained for two-man patrols and, when that demand was not met, bolstered the request with a campaign of advertisements in the media and letters to politicians, and took it to arbitration. In what appeared to be a direct reaction to public pressure, the arbitrator imposed dusk-to-dawn two-man cruisers on the Toronto force.[49]

Police personnel organizations are frequently involved in campaigns that are essentially political. Annually the police unions and associations urge a return to the death penalty (despite evidence that the homicide rate has not changed since Canada abandoned capital punishment), tougher sentencing by the courts, restrictions on parolees, and a host of other causes that go much beyond what one might term "working conditions." This is not bargaining with management but an attempt to influence the public and its leaders by conjuring up the spectre of crime. But should those who enforce the law attempt to influence those who make the law? The same kind of question arises with respect to teachers who lobby school boards and civic workers who influence city councils.

Police unions and organizations are hostile to management, in spite of the fact that management personnel are former members of those groups. The hostility is aggravated by the fact that police management is rarely skilled in management questions, making negotiations frustrating and bitter — the result being a tough and cohesive police association.[50]

Management-employee relations are structured somewhat differently in the RCMP. There is no formal police association, but divisional representatives are elected by officers to serve on a full-time basis for two or three years. These representatives meet frequently with each other and with management. There appear to be more relaxed relations between the two sides and a greater willingness by management to consider employee participation in decision making. The arrangement has been characterized as both a company union and an example of worker participatory democracy. In any event, RCMP officers do not appear to be any happier in their jobs than their municipal counterparts.

Private Policing

The discussion of the structure of police work up to this point has necessarily left out one aspect — the work done by private police. While it is commonly assumed that policing is a function exclusively carried out by public agencies and paid for by tax dollars, private policing is on the rise. In 1975, the latest year for which figures are available, there were 51,243 public police officers in Canada and 47,780 private officers. There is some thought that in the intervening years the number of private officers has surpassed the public.[51]

The term *private police* may not be entirely fair, since the functions provided by such individuals are limited almost entirely to the provision of security. The term *private security* might be more appropriate. Private security officers (or "security guards") perform general patrol functions on private property. Occasionally they call the public police to discuss a criminal occurrence, but this kind of information-sharing is not extensive. Private security officers are more concerned with loss and its prevention than they are about crime per se. They do not consider the question of blame, retribution or punishment to be of as much importance as prevention.

Private policing services are now so pervasive that we take them for granted. They operate in most large office buildings, in shopping centres, at sporting events, in libraries. Few question the powers or actions of security guards.

Several factors account for the growth in private policing since World War Two. First, some companies have grown exceedingly large, and their managers have concluded that it makes good sense to set up a company police force to achieve corporate ends. For instance, General Motors is thought to have the fifth-largest police force in the United States. While such monolithic firms set up their own policing to prevent loss, it is entirely possible that officers can be used to restore order and enforce various rules against employees and others. In the past, private policing companies like Pinkerton's have been used (as in Colorado on behalf of Rockefeller) to break strikes, using techniques including beating and killing strikers and their families.

Second, there has been a spectacular growth of what is called ''mass private property,'' property that is privately owned but which the public is encouraged to use. A shopping centre is a prime example. History helps to throw light on the distinction between public and private property.

Centuries ago, when roads were privately controlled, the king's highway was a novelty. It was the one highway to which the King's Peace was extended and over which the king promised safe passage. The King's Peace did not apply on private property, with one exception: inns. A traveller needed protection not only on the king's highway, but also where he stopped for food and rest. Thus, travellers' stops became known as public houses even though they were privately owned.

This distinction between the public and the private survived the Industrial Revolution. Police operated on public property, and landowners were responsible for their own property. The police were not allowed on private property except in very special circumstances: to prevent a crime, to arrest someone in flight from a crime, or when invited onto the property by the owner. These rules, of course, form the basis for police powers at the present time.

In the last thirty years, buildings have become larger, and huge complexes of buildings and walkways have developed in private ownership. The tradition of buildings having access from public streets has given way to buildings only having access from privately owned streets and other land. Shops face on a privately owned mall rather than a publicly owned street. Office buildings are so large that it is not difficult to get lost in the ''public'' hallways.

There is an ambivalence in the nature of this space. The owner of a shopping mall wishes to attract as many people as possible to his land, providing they are the right kind of people doing the right kind of thing. Owners of office buildings are delighted to have people in the lobby and on the elevators, since they are no doubt there for some legitimate commercial purpose. Yet as many teenagers know, the invitation to frequent a shopping mall is rarely extended to them. It is private property.

This is not a familiar form of private property like a backyard or a living room. And it is a different sort of space than a small private store. Its private nature is invisible: it functions as quite public space. Hence the name *mass private property*.

Because this space is privately owned, public police officers are not permitted to enter unless invited, chasing a suspect, preventing a crime, or having a court-authorized warrant to be there for some specific purpose, such as to conduct a search. To control "public" activities, the owner hires his own police force. Security guards watch carefully for those who do not seem to fit in or for those who might cause trouble. In most shopping malls, guards are told to challenge those who sit on a bench for more than five minutes.

The rights of the public in such space are circumscribed by the desires of the owner. Any form of politicking or other proselitizing will usually lead to speedy eviction. Picketing will also lead to expulsion, plus charges under the Petty Trespass Act. Since the property is privately rather than publicly owned, rights of free speech and public gatherings don't apply. The freedoms for which so many have fought so hard in the past do not exist on mass private property.

Because the job of the private security officer on mass private property is mostly preventative in nature, arrests are rarely made. When they are, it is usually with the consent of the accused, who is asked something like "Will you please come to my office?" Searches conducted at libraries, stores and sports events are almost always done with the consent of the party involved. Signs are posted indicating that searches may take place, and it is assumed that visitors to the property are consenting to this procedure. Uniforms worn by private officers help to evoke consent by giving the impression of authority and power.

The assumption made by a private officer about someone who refuses to permit a search is that this person should not be on the property, and that as the agent for the owner, the officer should force such a person to leave. Often the officer will have the person sign a document undertaking not to return, lest he or she be subject to arrest. The following is the document used by private security officers in one Toronto shopping mall:

> Whereas the management of College Park has decided that your presence is undesirable;
> Take notice that you are not to enter onto the premises of College Park, including the parking areas, and the Hayter Street Parkette, from this date forward without first obtaining the written permission of management, and that if you are found on the premises you will be liable to arrest by the College Park security staff and/or the Metropolitan Toronto Police and to prosecution under the Trespass to Property Act to the fullest extent of the law.

The notice is dated, addressed to the person in question, signed by the officer, and then signed in acknowledgement by the transgressor. There is no trial preceding the signing of this document, but simply a decision by a security officer to take action — another example of how traditional rights appear to have no place on mass private property.

Most provinces have legislation requiring private policing companies and their employees to be registered, but the standards and controls are minimal. There are no examinations inquiring into education, work experience, and drug or medical problems, and the sole criterion for acceptability is that the candidate be at least eighteen years old. Those who work for these companies bear out the loose job standards: many are part time, hold the job less than a year, and (according to one study) take the job because they are not qualified for or cannot find any other position.[52] What training occurs is usually on the job. Few private officers know when they are entitled to make an arrest.[53]

As in the other sectors of the economy, the ownership of private forces is concentrated in a few hands. Four firms employ 54 per cent of all security guards in Ontario, a low concentration compared with the United States, where seven firms employ 72 per cent of all guards. In Ontario, 43 per cent of all guards are employed by American security companies. Fortunately less than 4 per cent of all guards in Canada are armed, compared with 47 per cent in the States.[54]

Reviewing what we've seen thus far, there seem to be three important distinctions between private and public policing. Private policing is much more worried about crime and thus directs its energies to prevention rather than to crime conviction. Public police are worried about apprehension after an incident has occurred, although with the recent emphasis on foot patrol, the public police are seemingly mimicking the private.

Second, private police are not concerned with blame, retribution or punishment. The methods of adjudication they use are swift, informal and frequently muddled, and the punishments are often severe. At one Canadian university, a student may not receive a degree unless tickets for campus parking violations and other accounts are fully paid.

Third, there are few legal restraints on the private police officer and few rights available to the public. The assumption is that the public consents to whatever rules are made by the owner of the mass private property, and thus, on the basis of contract, the member of the public generally waives all rights. The contrast to the constraints on a public police officer and the rights available in a public place is considerable.

These differences between public and private forces raise difficult questions about the nature of policing. For instance, more and more homeowners are installing private alarm systems that ring in a police station. In Toronto in 1981 these alarms rang more than 400,000 times. The police responded to 2,000, assuming the rest were set off in error. This activity resulted in the arrest of exactly one suspect. In all probability, the police will soon refuse to be hooked into such alarm systems, simply because of the expense. Private security companies can be expected to offer a package where they respond to private alarms on a fee-for-service basis. How will these private officers arrive at the scene of the call. Armed? In great numbers? Will they negotiate with the suspects? Who protects the rights of the intruder, whatever those rights might be?

There are other, more basic questions raised by the public/private quandary:

- Is private policing pointing in a useful direction by discarding blame and retribution, and worrying more about prevention? As we've seen, public police base much of their activity on the assumption that catching a wrongdoer deters others from similar actions, but that assumption may either be false, extremely expensive, or both.
- The controls on police powers extend only to public police. Are these controls really an expression of our fear of the power of the state — or are they directed specifically at those who wish to enforce codes of behaviour? If the latter, should limitations

on police powers be applied to private forces as well?

- Could society reduce its reliance on the public police to some extent without suffering ill effects? Many equate a police presence with social order. Could private officers be substituted to secure this benefit?

As the public purse becomes more strained, these questions may become more pointed. In 1982 one Toronto municipality hired private security guards to ensure public safety in its parks after being told that extra public officers would not be provided for this service. Retaining private police was a much less expensive solution. Will this arrangement become more commonplace?

The modern police force had its origins in the measures taken by the private shippers to protect their property along and on the Thames River. The benefits were so great that the public sector quickly took control. The growth of the public forces responded to the very great strains that society was facing thanks to the Industrial Revolution. As the twentieth century comes to a close, the modern corporation has become more dominant in shaping our existence. Perhaps this latest economic transformation of society will dictate that a private police force would be entirely acceptable to most people.

But this change — from public to private — raises the questions about what the police are really trying to do and what public expectations are. These are the questions we turn to in the next chapter.

4
Philosophies of Policing

Like the question of what police really do and the debate about the nature of crime, the issues involved in settling on a police role in society are thorny and complex. This chapter reviews police goals and objectives and then goes on to the related subjects of productivity, police powers and the exercise of discretion, and models of police governance.

What Are the Police Trying to Do?

The definition of the duties and powers of a police officer given in the Police Act of Ontario is typical of the wording across the country. The officer is charged with:

- preserving the peace;
- preventing robberies and other crimes and offences;
- apprehending offenders;
- laying informations before the proper tribunals; and
- prosecuting and aiding in the prosecution of offenders.

These few words define the police function almost wholly in terms of crime: catching and prosecuting criminals or trying to prevent crime. There is no mention of traffic control, helping people who can't look after themselves, or indeed any social role. If police were to be judged entirely on performance of this statutory role, they would get poor marks, since most crimes are never solved. Certainly in the public's mind the police are crime fighters. Dressed in a quasi-military uniform, equipped with a club and a gun, the police are assumed to stand between the law-abiding and the lawbreakers. The police battle crime on behalf of society.

But this image, reinforced by countless movies and television shows, is misleading. Less than 15 per cent of an officer's time is spent dealing with crime.[1] There are many other tasks police are called on to perform, such as responding to non-criminal emergencies.

A different definition of police work is that police maintain law and order. But "law and order" is not an indivisible whole. It is most difficult to maintain order while upholding the law. Individual rights will almost always be infringed in the maintenance of order, since the latter always implies putting someone in their place. Imagine the paradox of the officer at the rock concert — drug arrests (enforcing the law) will lead to a melee (disorder). Does he opt for law or order? Conversely, concern about legal rights may often produce disorder in a crisis. Imagine an officer taking the time to explain rights to a bank robber as he is being arrested on the sidewalk.

This conundrum has to do with the very nature of *law* and *order*. Law acts as a restraint on police activity, and minimizes the chance of convicting an innocent person. Laws protect people from the abuse of official power and attempt to establish a framework for judicial decision making that is impartial and consistent. In contrast, the idea of order implies freedom from violence and unknown threats, and the subservience of the individual to some kind of social order. Police are asked to act to ensure our safety and security, and society prizes these results above the law.

In Canada in particular, the maintenance of order seems paramount. Many believe that the North West Mounted Police were sent to the Prairies to secure order so that liberty would then follow. Canada has even established a tradition of freeing the rebels once order is restored. William Lyon Mackenzie, the leaders of the Winnipeg General Strike of 1919, and the conspirators in the 1970 October Crisis have all been made into heroes of some sort. This pattern has become a hallmark of Canadian values, and the police role has become so pervasive that traditions have developed permitting police — in the name of securing order — to break into private property, steal, open mail and publish fraudulent information.[2]

Further shattering the unity of "law and order" is the fact that order means different things to different people. Keeping order in front of the American consulate in any Canadian city could mean that demonstrations are not allowed or that demonstrations are allowed providing that they are peaceful.

A third definition of the police function is embodied in the words "serve and protect." The motto of the Toronto police force is "to serve and protect." In Chicago it is "serve and protect," in Minneapolis "to serve, to protect." These words are overused. Their ambiguity lies in the question of who is to be served and who is to be protected.

One school of thought on the radical left holds that police serve and protect those in power and that they will enforce policies perpetuating class, race and sexual oppression.[3] The state, the argument goes, is the major perpetrator of crime. Many episodes are dredged up to support this view — the theft of land from Natives, the internment of Japanese Canadians during World War Two and of Quebecois during the 1970 October Crisis. Police act as agents of the state and carry on doing these same sorts of things on an everyday basis, although not spectacularly — intervening in strikes on the side of management, for example, and arresting picketers.

Others argue that the police act not just for the interests of those in power, but also as agents of social control. The law exists, so goes the theme, to give the police the means to maintain social order. The criminal law is a small and limited tool for this purpose, and occasionally police must take matters into their own hands to impose the kind of control that they think is necessary and would be expected by society at large.

Toronto police raided bathhouses frequented by homosexuals in early 1981, causing substantial damage, both physical and psychological. The police rationale for the raids — that organized crime was involved in the bathhouses — has never been shown to have any basis in fact. Many have concluded that police simply decided to take action they thought appropriate, action they suspected would be tolerated by the public even though it exceeded acknowledged police authorizations. Apparently they were correct, since there were no reprimands for these raids. Police frequently intervene against those who might be considered troublesome, as judged by the clothes they wear (punkers, bikers), their colour (blacks, particularly Rastafarians), or sexual orientation (homosexuals).

This theory of social control might be one way of explaining ''police riots,'' where police engage in beatings and overreactive behaviour such as the Morrish Road incident in Scarborough, Ontario, in 1982. There, some fifty officers systematically beat young people at a party in the early hours of the morning. In spite of lengthy investigations by the Police Complaints Board, not one officer who participated in the melee has been identified. The police rioted and then closed ranks to protect each other.[4] Given the scant adverse public reaction to such incidents, police again might imagine that they are tacitly being given a free hand to do as they please.

In their attempt to maintain control with little training and few tools, the police stretch their mandate to the limit with more weaponry and technology — leading to the 1977 newspaper photo of the chief of police in Toronto looking down the barrel of a bazooka at the reader. Making the police responsible for maintaining law and order might very well lead to the belief by the police that they are the main — and independent — agents of social control.

Police can be crime fighters, maintainers of law and order, or agents of social control. A fourth definition of police activities links them directly to the criminal justice system. Yet, as noted earlier, the bulk of police resources are not directed against crime. Any quick examination of a police force's structure bears this out. O.W. Wilson, author of the influential book *Police Administration*, divides police functions into service administration and law administration. The former provides round-the-clock service for emergencies, first aid, directing traffic, helping people in trouble, and referral to other services. This is the "helping" function.

Law administration includes the maintenance of order, both controlling crisis situations and preventing major criminal outbursts, and law enforcement, encompassing the detection of crime and the apprehension of criminals. Wilson's description of police activities is set out in the following diagram.

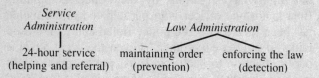

Only the detection function is part of the criminal justice system. The others relate to different parts of the social structure. The bulk of police resources are given to patrol, which is concerned mostly with prevention (on the questionable assumption that visibility leads to deterrence). No police resources are directly assigned to the helping function, although all officers are expected to fill this role in day-to-day activities.

Some scholars — like Jerome Skolnick — argue that police are more occupied with a justice system of their own creation than with the independent criminal justice system. Arrest, incarceration and questioning are police activities that occur before any reference is made to charges, judges or courts, and these actions are of greatest influence on the behaviour of the suspect and, subsequently, the disposition of the case. Given the great proportion of cases resolved by guilty plea, the role of the court system can be seen as little more than confirming police actions and police justice. One Canadian study notes that "many more people are detained prior to trial than are jailed after sentence,"[5] a revealing indication of the control exercised by police in the face of a neutral justice system. Thus, it can be strongly argued that police functions are not so much part of the criminal justice system as that system is an adjunct to the police-run justice system.[6]

When pressed on what goals they have, police authorities often turn to the principles elucidated by Sir Robert Peel in 1829, when he introduced legislation to establish the first modern police force in the English-speaking world. The principles (outlined in chapter 1) stress the congruity of police and societal goals. Peel's principles have gained common currency. For example, they are scattered throughout the 1979 annual report of the Vancouver police. The Peel phrase ''The public are the police and the police are the public'' was used as the title of a study of policing in Ontario during the 1970s. Quotations from Peel are frequently cited by police authorities as the basis for judging police actions.

Unfortunately, Peel's principles are rooted in the times they were enunciated — perhaps they might even have been outdated then by several centuries — and are not easily transposed over the years. For instance, the first principle (''to prevent crime and disorder, as an alternative to their repression by military force and by the severity of legal punishment'') is a clear reference to the fact that English police would not be a standing army, which is how the English viewed the French gendarmes. The notion that the police might exist today in place of any occupying army is not one that would find favour in any quarter in Canada (although the two came together in the 1970 October Crisis in Quebec).

Many of Peel's principles are directed towards police behaviour that will secure a compliant public, with an assumption that the police are there to ''secure observance of law'' or ''restore order.'' The reference to the public/police relationship is a historical footnote: for six hundred years in law — if not in practice — all members of society were required to perform policing duties by rote. That rule had disappeared at least two hundred years before Peel introduced this legislation. In sum, the Peel principles are of little help in explaining the function of policing in the latter half of the twentieth century.

The American scholar Herman Goldstein has used a different approach to define police goals and objectives. Working with the American Bar Association, he looked at the actual work police do, and gauged public response. He arrived at eight objectives:

1. To prevent and control conduct widely recognized as threatening to life and property (serious crime).

2. To aid individuals who are in danger of physical harm, such as the victim of a criminal attack, or of an accident.

3. To protect constitutional guarantees, such as the right of free speech and assembly.

4. To facilitate the movement of people and vehicles.

5. To assist those who cannot care for themselves; the intoxicated, the addicted, the mentally ill, the physically disabled, the old and the young.

6. To resolve conflict, whether it be between individuals, groups of individuals or individuals and their government.

7. To identify problems that have the potential of becoming more serious problems for the individual citizen, for the police, or for the government.

8. To create and maintain a feeling of security in the community.[7]

It is fair to say that these kinds of objectives, perhaps with modifications appropriate to Canada or a specific Canadian city, set out the kinds of tasks expected from the contemporary police force. Inevitably, these objectives occasionally are in conflict, requiring choices about which objective has priority in a given instance. But that is a human problem, with human solutions.

There appear to be several reasons why police forces have not, to date, outlined objectives in the manner of Goldstein. First, embracing this sort of job description would involve a loss of status in comparison with simply "fighting crime." Many of the tasks are unexciting, without the drama of danger, violence and fighting the forces of evil on behalf of a grateful society. Second, officers are not trained to deliver these kinds of services; they are trained to fight crime. It would be unusual for a group of civil servants to declare publicly that they are performing jobs for which they aren't trained.

Politicians too have not been clear about a role for the police and have not been willing to discuss police objectives in a straightforward manner, as Goldstein did. To do so could expose the politician to an avalanche of criticism that he was being "soft on crime" or that he wanted to turn police officers into social workers.

Even with tight budgets, sufficient funds for policing have always been found by politicians. It has not been necessary to ask tough questions. As the financial situation becomes more difficult for municipalities due to reduced transfer payments from provincial governments, one can expect politicians and police commissioners to develop a clearer focus on police objectives in order to cut "fat" from the force.

Measuring Police Productivity and Efficiency

Measuring productivity in policing is a daunting task, given the difficulties of even defining police roles and functions. As a reaction, simple numerical measures have been sought. The "clearance rate" is one of the most frequently used measures. It tries to account for the disposition of every incident reported to the police. If the incident is resolved in some fashion — whether informally by the complainant agreeing that nothing can be done or formally by laying a charge — then the incident is "cleared." If there is no resolution, then it is not cleared. Quite simply, if the occurrence sheet gets off the officer's desk, the incident is cleared.

Clearance rates are a prominent feature of police annual reports. In the case of the Hamilton-Wentworth police, the clearance rate has varied in the last few years between 40 and 45 per cent. For drug offences in 1982 it was 99 per cent, for thefts 17 per cent, indicating the difference between what the police know and what action they can take. Clearance rates like these are typical of large forces in Canada.

Unfortunately, the clearance rate isn't a measure of much of anything. An incident will be cleared if the complainant agrees to drop it. And it will be cleared if the officer unilaterally decides to simply file it as insoluble. Some incidents don't have a fair story line to them, leaving the officer with a complainant who can never be satisfied.

Further, the clearance rate fails to take account of preventative actions, conflict resolution, directing traffic, helping the helpless, and all of the important social roles police are expected to play. The clearance rate is a failure as a measurement of police performance.

A second measure frequently used in judging police efficiency is response time — the time it takes to respond to a call. The assumption is that speed is critical both to solve the problem and to give customer satisfaction. Yet as noted in chapter 2, neither assumption is true. Further, this index — like the clearance rate — fails to deal with police work not triggered by calls from the public. This method too is unsatisfactory as a measure of police productivity.

Any blueprint for a more effective measurement must begin by grappling with the central problem of objectives. One writer suggests five different areas of work:[8]

- Crime prevention: personal crime; property crime; selected crime
- Crime control: public reporting to police; case closure (solution); case preparation and testimony; stolen property return; constitutional propriety; custody of prisoners
- Conflict resolution: interpersonal conflict; intergroup conflict; personal stress
- General service: traffic; miscellaneous services to the public; auxiliary services to the criminal justice system; communication with the public
- Police administration: police integrity; community leadership; coordination with other agencies

This list indicates the diversity of tasks to be done, and highlights the difficulty in deciding when jobs are done well. Some efforts are easy to calibrate, such as the number of prisoners who escape police custody. But for others, the problems are immense. It is almost impossible to measure the efficiency of interpersonal conflict resolution except on a case-by-case basis. The number of times police attend such conflicts, and the frequency of physical harm, can be noted easily, but the cumulative effectiveness of police intervention is a subjective measure not easily generalized.

The headings listed above can be broken down one step further to provide a fuller picture of the challenge of measuring productivity. Take the initial subcategory of preventing personal crime, that is, crime against the person. The following is a very precise statement of objectives:

> To minimize the number of those major violent crimes against persons (homicide, rape, robbery, assault causing bodily harm) that are preventable under the following circumstances:
>   in public; in commercial industrial establishments that are police hazards; or, in situations where police assistance could have been provided in time to prevent a crime or an escalation of an incident to a crime;
>   as estimated from crimes reported to the police. [9]

Unfortunately, the measure is very complicated. There is no sense asking police to prevent occurrences that have not come to their attention or that they could not be expected to be aware of. The measure of success will be the ability of the police to predict in advance exactly what kinds of things might occur and where, and on the basis of such prognostications, construct an effective preventative program. Only then can the productivity of programs preventing personal crime be fairly assessed.

To get a full portrait of productivity, similar complicated objectives would be required for all other areas of police work, along with further estimates. This difficult process will not give any handy rule of thumb by which to measure the efficiency and productivity of a police force. Small wonder police turn to clearance rates and response times as touchstones.

Part of the problem in measuring productivity is that to a large extent the police function is response to the actions of others. If society has determined that everyone is entitled to carry a gun, then the blame for a high incidence of shootings cannot be laid at the doorstep of the police force. Police can play a useful role in suggesting programs to minimize certain incidents, such as car accidents, but those programs might not be acceptable politically. An example is the practice of stopping a great many drivers for random checks. Thus, the limitations of measuring productivity can be attributed in part to the fact that expectations of police intervention are not entirely agreed upon in society. And there are significant differences of opinion about whether police should be a strictly reactive force or whether proactive intervention should be encouraged. We are again back at the dilemma of maintaining order versus upholding the law.

Productivity could be treated in a much narrower sense by measuring various indices that do not question the functions performed. One such measure is the number of calls for service, measured per officer, per unit or per shift. Some forces work on an average of four calls per officer per shift, others more. While many calls might take a few minutes (kids playing hockey on the street), some might take considerably longer (a hostage-taking incident could last a day or two). But over a period of a year, reasonable assumptions about the length of a call for service can probably be made. Some forces are bound by collective agreements requiring two officers in a car after dusk, and in these cases it is fairer to compare not calls per officer, but calls per unit.

These kinds of measurement help with comparisons between forces. If one force can handle ten calls per officer per shift, then a force with a lower ratio might look to improvements, such as by referring more calls to other agencies, having officers spend less time with complainants, and so forth. This measure might show that more energy is being spent satisfying callers than solving problems.

Rather than measure calls for service, the index could be incidents or charges per officer, as noted in chapter 3. Is Vancouver, with seventy-one charges per officer per year, more efficient than Toronto, with thirty-nine charges per officer? Should charges be laid simply to keep up this statistic? Is an officer ''soft'' if his charge ratio is lower than the force's as a whole, or is he better because he is able to bring about non-criminal resolutions more frequently? Dependence on this measure could increase reliance on quotas, already an entrenched police management tool (whereby, for example, the number of parking tickets and moving violations chalked up by each officer is reviewed monthly). Obviously, numerical measures of this sort make sense only if police objectives are previously agreed on.

Another measure of productivity is the efficiency of the use of police personnel. Manpower should be matched to workload; the number of officers on duty at any one time should correspond to the amount of work police will be called on to perform. This is a simple measure of productivity in any bureaucracy. In an Ontario Police Commission study of eight of the largest police forces in Southern Ontario, it was found that ''only one of eight forces...had adopted a shift scheduling system which permitted manpower to closely match the call for service pattern over a 24-hour period and through the week.''[10] This is a relatively straightforward management problem which, if resolved, could substantially increase productivity.

The other side of the shift-scheduling coin is deployment, or how officers are used in their jobs. The Kansas City study described in chapter 3 indicates that random police activities like patrol accomplish little — it would be more productive if police officers were given specific tasks.

Directing the random activities of patrol is known as "target hardening." The officer is told who he should be after, what places he should watch, and what he should be on the lookout for. In some areas of police work, target hardening is thought to increase productivity and actually result in the prevention of crime.[11]

Deployment questions can also arise in regard to calls for service. Should all calls be responded to? Should calls be categorized so that important calls get dealt with first? For instance, when a bicycle is reported stolen, virtually all the police can do is record the serial number and inform the complainant if the bike falls into police hands. Chances of recovering the bike itself are small. In these circumstances, should police go to the caller or should the caller come to the police? Isn't it a waste of police resources to send officers to a complainant's home to take a report? Couldn't the complainant be told to come to the station instead? And of calls regarding violence, which should get priority — those where violence is occurring or those where it might break out? How is the recipient of a call to make a distinction? Many forces are experimenting with different approaches to these questions, usually finding that some of the calls being responded to with patrol cars can just as easily be dealt with over the telephone.

The effectiveness of police investigation and crime analysis is rarely questioned, perhaps because it is not too visible, perhaps because it touches too closely on fears about crime. But a 1975 study in the United States casts considerable doubt on the efficiency of the current criminal investigation process. The study looked at many large American forces and concluded that the detective function left much to be desired. Some conclusions of the study are:[12]

- More than half of all serious reported crimes receive no more than superficial attention from all investigators.
- An investigator's time is mainly taken up in work on cases that experience indicates will not be solved.
- For solved cases, the investigator spends more time on post-arrest processing than on the pre-arrest phase.
- The single most important determinant of whether a case will be solved is the information the victim supplies to the immediately responding patrol officer. In other words, the key information is that obtained by the officer on the scene, not by the detective.
- Of solved cases in which the offender is not identifiable at the time of the initial report, almost all were cleared as a result of routine police procedures. Tricks apparently have a low yield.
- In many departments, investigators do not consistently and thoroughly document the key evidentiary facts, with untoward consequences for prosecutors.

While the study is American, it was done by a reputable organization and was broadly enough based to suggest that many of its conclusions could also apply to Canadian police forces.

One common suggestion for increasing police productivity is civilianization, or the replacement of police officers with other employees who have received no special police training. This approach recognizes that many jobs need not be carried out by someone with expensively obtained police skills. Areas such as payroll, auto mechanics and maintaining communication systems have had a strong civilian component for some years. More recently, civilians are being used for functions such as lost and found and courtroom duty, and there are some suggestions they might be used for investigating minor accidents.

Some suggestions for productivity improvements are easier to implement and measure than others. But in the area of police functions and objectives, there is widespread feeling that there are no easy and reasonable answers. Two English writers suggest that further research into productivity improvement in crime prevention might simply conclude that "the crime prevention value of a police force rests less on precisely what it does than on the symbolic belief in its effectiveness."[13] The former chief of the Calgary police force has stated: "I'd like to offer the minority view that many, if not most, of the important elements which go to make up an effective police service may not be measurable, at least not in a manner that is objective, and comparable."[14]

Another writer approaches this question from a different angle:

> The quality of work done probably varies inversely with the amount of work undertaken. If a cost-conscious public purse requires the police to produce voluminous figures of, for example, service calls undertaken or arrests made in order to justify police budgets then it is clear that there will be a greatly increased danger of quantity in all cases pushing out quality. To introduce the quality element into our measures of "work done," questions will have to be asked about what, if any, analysis of calls is being undertaken and with what result, if any, use is being

made of computers to police areas which were not traditionally policed with any degree of regularity or success by prior methods....The call for "productivity" must not result in a headlong rush to simply produce more of the same for the same price.[15]

The key to productivity and efficiency changes lies in observation and experimentation, two basic management tools that are not pursued with great enthusiasm by Canadian forces. The Metro Toronto force allocated less than $400,000 of a $300-million budget in 1984 to planning and research. Most other Canadian forces do not even have an allocation for planning and research.

One exception to this rule is the Edmonton force, which for the last ten years has had on staff a director of organizational studies. The position is filled by a civilian with an academic background, who secured funds in 1982 to study innovation in American police forces. The result of the study is the CATCH (Criminal Activities Traced, Confined and Halted) program, being implemented in early 1985. CATCH will permit officers to investigate most cases themselves rather than turning them over to detectives, saving duplication of effort while boosting morale; screening cases to ensure that investigative energy is devoted to cases which have the best chance of being solved; reducing and more effectively managing patrol; and better managing investigations by analyzing information and procedures. The results of these experiments will be carefully monitored to determine their effectiveness, both in cost and policing terms.

Questions about productivity and efficiency always come down to whether existing tasks can be done as well or better for less money. Experimentation is one of the few methods of determining whether improvements can be made in various areas, but unless productivity is seen as an important problem area and unless funds are allocated for experimentation, it is difficult to see how useful changes will be made.

Discretion and Implied Powers

The officer out on patrol daily comes up against the fact that some objectives are in conflict. In a given situation — which may be heated — he must decide what objectives will be pursued (will he enforce the law or will he preserve order?) and how that objective will be most easily achieved. He must decide whom he is going to please most: his chief? his colleagues? the disputants? the public? the media? The choice he makes is the exercise of police discretion at the street level.

The use of discretion is central to police work, as indeed it is to most important undertakings. This fact leads to many citizen complaints of "Why was I treated differently from everyone else?" Police authorities do not like to admit that they make discretionary decisions, preferring to say they are simply doing their duty or enforcing the law. But their tasks by their nature require discretion.

The officer on patrol must continually use his discretion. But before he leaves the station, administrative decisions are made affecting how police services are delivered. These decisions are also discretionary in nature. They can be divided into three levels.

First, where should policing monies be spent? Should the youth squad be beefed up and the mounted squad phased out? Should money be taken from patrol work to be used for research and development? Are certain kinds of crime prevention worth spending money on? Questions such as these are usually decided within the police bureaucracy, although the public is now asking more frequently that they be debated publicly.

Second, with general spending priorities decided, how should resources be deployed? Should officers be put on the street to deal with drug-related matters, or should informers be retained to gather basic information? Should more emphasis be put on foot patrols and less on car patrols? Should crimes involving prostitution be dealt with by publicizing the names of those arrested, or should energy be directed to increasing the number of arrests?

The third order of administrative decision making occurs on a daily basis. Where should patrols be emphasized tonight? What police objectives should be pursued at the rock concert tomorrow evening when sizable quantities of drugs are expected to be consumed?

These kinds of decisions are made by police managers, from the chief through to staff inspectors. In some cases the police commission takes responsibility for them. In certain situations — street prostitution is the best example — the public has shown growing interest in how police make decisions about the deployment of forces and the kinds of criminal charges to be pursued. However, police authorities have acted in a haphazard fashion, sometimes (as in Vancouver in early 1984) raiding "escort" services at the very time when citizens wanted to push prostitution off the streets and into hotel rooms. Police are uneasy talking publicly about this area of decision making and have tried to be all things to all people. If the financial position of municipalities continues to deteriorate, cutbacks in police service must be expected, and these cuts will provoke public debate on what services should be provided where.

The questions decided by police discretion are seldom easy. The 1982 Clifford Olson case in British Columbia is a case in point. The RCMP decided to pay Olson's family $100,000 in exchange for his revealing the graves of youths he had murdered. From a police point of view, including both economy in gathering information and the likelihood of success, it was a good decision. Getting Olson to point out the graves was better than a signed confession. That action virtually secured convictions in court, while the most carefully prepared circumstantial evidence gathered at an expense of hundreds of thousands of dollars might have failed on a technicality.

But from the media and some members of the public there was a moral outrage. It seemed Olson was being rewarded for owning up to heinous crimes. The two groups — the police and the public — had different objectives, and thus different ways of looking at the situation. If the objective was to get the best evidence by the quickest legal means possible, the police succeeded. Apparently, others thought that an equally important objective was that the killer's family not benefit.

There is an almost bewildering array of choices available to a patrol officer who is about to intervene in a situation. Each form of intervention affects the objectives that can be obtained. The following police actions are possible in the most mundane of incidents:[16]

- Stop and question.
- Conduct an investigation.
- Conduct a frisk.
- Take person into custody for investigation.

- Take person into custody for his own protection.
- Issue an order to desist.
- Issue an order to leave.
- Issue an order to move on.
- Issue a caution.
- Threaten to use force.
- Use force.

In a complicated situation, such as a domestic dispute where a couple have come to blows, an officer might use many of these techniques, as well as considering whether a domestic response team should be called in. The choices are both important and difficult.

Discretion is also applied in the disposition of an occurrence. Quite clearly the form of intervention strongly influences what will happen next. If the officer responding to a domestic dispute enters the apartment with gun drawn, there is little likelihood that the dispute will be resolved with a friendly chat or a warning. If the intervention has a softer edge, then the range of choices available to the officer is more extensive, ranging from charges and arrests to warnings and cautions. Sometimes the determining factor is timing: an officer can usually agree to abandon the completion of a parking ticket if the car owner comes along before the licence plate number is filled in — after that point, the matter is out of the officer's control.

Like discretionary decisions about intervention, those surrounding disposition are left to the individual officer. While in most bureaucracies discretion is reserved for those in a senior decision-making capacity, in policing much of the leeway filters down to rank-and-file officers — those at the lowest level of the structure.

The discretionary role of the patrol officer evolved from common law and is best exemplified in a 1968

English court case. The police chief sent a memorandum to all officers stating that charges should not be laid against London gambling clubs unless there were allegations of cheating and the like. A citizen brought an application to force the police to enforce the law. Lord Denning, one of England's most influential judges, refused the request, stating:

> It is the duty of every Chief Constable to enforce the law of the land. He must decide whether or not suspected persons are to be prosecuted and, if need be, bring the prosecution or see that it is brought; but in all these things he is not the servant of anyone, save of the law itself. No minister of the crown can tell him that…he must or must not prosecute this man or that one. Nor can any police authority tell him so. The responsibility of law enforcement lies on him. He is answerable to the law and the law alone.[17]

This idea was developed further by Madam Justice Mitchell of the Supreme Court of the State of South Australia as cited by the McDonald Commission report on the RCMP. Commenting on Lord Denning's decision, she goes further:

> No government can properly direct any policeman to prosecute or not to prosecute any particular person or class of persons although it is not unknown for discussion between the executive and the police to lead to an increase or abatement of prosecution for certain types of offences. That is not to say that the Commissioner of Police is in any way bound to follow government direction in relation to prosecutions. Nor should it be so. There are many police functions in respect of which it would be unthinkable for the government to intervene. It is easier to cite examples than to formulate a definition of the circumstances in which the

Commissioner of Police alone should have responsibility for the operation of the police force.[18]

These approaches — which separate quite clearly the law-making function from the law enforcement function, a distinction praised by Charles Reith — also enshrine in the police force, and then in the individual officer, unfettered discretion.

Discretion is not learned at the police college, or in the operating manual, or from the rules and regulations. It is learned by watching other officers and seeing what they are rewarded for. If the custom of a particular force is to be tough on members of motorcycle gangs, then an officer can expect that he should be tough on bikers if he wants to move up in the force. If the force is in a city with a strong union presence, then the successful officer can be expected to overlook infractions on the picket line. The officer learns how to exercise discretion by seeing what his colleagues consider to be good and bad behaviour and by reading the political situation as best he can. Politicians make it known that they do not want Sunday-opening laws enforced too strictly, nor social gambling entirely prohibited, and police respond accordingly.

A change of precedent in a force can have dramatic results. In Toronto in the late 1970s, police were in the habit of shooting and killing suspects who had been trapped in their homes. In one thirteen-month period ending in September, 1979, Toronto police killed eight people this way. The killing of Albert Johnston produced such an outcry that the police decided to intervene in less violent ways, and for the next sixteen months not a single individual was killed by Toronto police. Instead of shooting, police "waited out" suspects.

There are several other factors besides internal patterns that influence police discretion. One is public opinion. Professional hockey players are rarely arrested for assaults during games because officers realize that such arrests will accomplish little and might bring the police into some criticism for restraining the gladiators. When a Toronto officer charged a New York Yankee baseball player with cruelty to animals for hitting a seagull with a baseball during an American league game in Toronto, the leading police commissioner, Metro Chairman Paul Godfrey, issued a public apology to the player and the charge was withdrawn.

In cases like the ones mentioned above, there is nothing devious or unsavoury about officers not enforcing the law. The public complaint is that there is uncertainty about how different officers will act in similar situations and whether the decisions made will be fair to all concerned. These are the two problem areas in the exercise of police discretion: equity and similarity of treatment.

At the present time, there are few internal police guidelines to ensure that officers in the same force approach the use of discretion in the same way. Where they exist, the guidelines usually evolve from a specialized police service such as the youth squad or domestic response team. For patrol officers there are no written guides to discretion, simply what the officer can pick up by osmosis from the actions of his colleagues.

Many critics have argued that police discretion should be structured, put into a pattern, for the guidance of officers and to satisfy public demand. K.C. Davis argues that five steps should be taken:[19]

- Admit that police do not enforce all laws all the

time, an admission that is easier said than done. Society must be honest enough to admit that the police do not have a duty to always enforce the law: some laws are enforced some of the time.

- Agree that the selective enforcement of laws should be open for all to see. Society should debate when laws should be enforced, and while a total and complete picture can never be agreed upon, some useful guidelines could emerge.
- Senior officers should be made responsible for devising policies about the exercise of discretion. General rules should be set out in writing.
- These guidelines should receive wide public discussion, including discussion by the officers who will be following them, before being adopted by management.
- Patrol officers should follow these guidelines.

Structuring discretion in this manner would involve discussions about present police practices and in all likelihood would result in control over the absolute discretionary power that police now feel they wield as a powerful tool. To date, no Canadian force has ventured into structuring discretion in this way.

Officers' freedom to use their discretion does empower them, and their power is enhanced by further *implied* powers. In the case of dispositions, legal police powers are actually quite limited. They are narrowly and exclusively defined by the criminal justice system (although people often assume police powers are much more extensive). Police have power to arrest, but only if the suspect is committing an indictable offence such as theft, robbery or something more serious, or if the officer thinks the suspect is fleeing from the commission of an offence.[20] An arrest occurs when the suspect feels that he is not free to go his own way. There are a host of borderline cases (when is a person effectively under arrest?), but the power of arrest without consent is narrow. Yet police power is broader than the letter of the law. When an arrest is not possible, the officer always asks if the suspect will get into the car or come voluntarily down to the station to talk. An agreeable suspect will place himself in a compromising position by getting into the cruiser where conditions are similar to being under arrest and the psychological position of the police is much improved. No strong-arm tactics are needed in these instances.

A warrant for arrest can be obtained from a justice of the peace on oath that there are reasonable and probable grounds for thinking a suspect has committed an offence. This power of arrest usually flows from a lengthy investigation, and the arrest is usually made by a detective.

The police also have the power to search both the person and property. While common law holds that a person under arrest may be searched, others may be searched only if suspected of carrying weapons or restricted drugs. Buildings may be searched without a warrant only if the officer has reasonable and probable grounds for believing that an offence is being committed. Most property searches are accompanied by a warrant obtained from a justice of the peace who has been convinced that evidence of a crime or a suspect will be found in the search.

These formal police powers of search and arrest are augmented by the ability of the police to use whatever force is necessary in the course of duty. The courts have interpreted this power very broadly, even exculpating an officer who shot dead a suspect fleeing from an automobile thought to be stolen. Police also have a very strong residual power, the power to arrest those considered to be "obstructing police." This power is often used to arrest those who do not obey police requests to move on, particularly at strike picket lines and demonstrations. Police need only find an order not obeyed to effect an arrest.

But the key police powers flow from gaining the consent of the suspect. He agrees to come into the cruiser or down to the station, where he is effectively under arrest. He agrees to a search of his residence on the assumption that if he resists, police will take punitive action of some sort. Thus, the *implied* authority of the police is the major power exercised over suspects.

Complicating matters, the police are in the invidious situation of having to adapt criminal justice powers to social situations where criminal activity is absent; they must find other responses where the application of these powers would be inappropriate. Deciding how to intervene, the objectives to be pursued, and the power to be invoked are all complex choices. It is this kind of decision that a patrol officer must make on a daily basis.

Governing the Police

The power to revise the police approach to police discretion — or any other aspect of administration and behaviour — lies in part with police governing bodies. In Canada police are governed in a myriad of ways. When police power was first formulated in the Town of York in 1834, power and authority to regulate policing belonged solely to the town council. Policing was seen to be such an integral part of governing the municipality that elected members of the town council had the power to arrest, as well as a free hand to sentence and imprison. The mayor and aldermen constituted the Mayor's Court, and the municipality was responsible for the local administration of justice.[21]

In 1849, with the passage of the Baldwin Act (precursor to the Municipal Act), local control of policing was confirmed for all Upper Canadian municipalities. Nine years later, the Municipal Institutions of Upper Canada Act required police to be controlled by a Board of Commissioners of Police consisting of the mayor, the recorder (a kind of secretary) and a police magistrate. Since both the recorder and the police magistrate were positions filled by provincial appointment, control of the board and thus the police was passed into the hands of the province. The requirement of a board did not apply to smaller municipal jurisdictions.

Why this shift to provincial control was enacted is still not clear. It may have been an attempt to reduce favouritism by town councils, or a response to poor administration. Whatever the explanation, the changes made in 1858 have remained in place in Ontario. Boards of Commissioners of Police continue to control police in large cities, with a majority of members appointed by provincial authorities. Towns and smaller cities have direct control of their own police. The requirement that one member of the board be a magistrate survived as late as 1979. Board membership first expanded from three to five in 1956, when the Metro Toronto police force was forged out of a number of smaller forces. The province appoints three of the five.

In the rest of Canada, the idea of a Board of Commissioners is not viewed so favourably. With the exception of the Montreal Urban Community, the idea is not employed in Quebec. Police boards have never existed in Newfoundland, and are required in Manitoba only for Winnipeg and Brandon. Moncton, Fredericton and St. John are the only New Brunswick communities that must have boards, and only the larger municipalities in Nova Scotia have them. They are not used in Prince Edward Island except in Charlottetown. Boards are required for all municipalities in British Columbia and Saskatchewan, and for larger centres in Alberta.

The size of boards and the method of appointing their members vary considerably. In Regina, the board's membership is the mayor and two aldermen; in Winnipeg, the mayor, two aldermen and two citizens appointed by council; in Calgary, three aldermen and four citizens appointed by council; and in Toronto, the metropolitan chairman, one member of Metro Council, two citizens and a judge appointed by the province. Thus, there are differences about the number of elected politicians, as well as who (politicians or citizens) gets the majority of the appointments. There does not seem

The following table (pp. 168-69) shows the great variety of approaches to police boards in Canada, the United States and Britain.[22] The present-day English system even incorporates the Watch Committee, a concept springing from the Statute of Westminster of 1285.

Police boards have the normal functions of a governing body: budget preparation and control; collective bargaining; rules and regulations; recruitment, promotions, suspensions and dismissals; internal discipline and complaints; and general policy. But what is remarkable is the fact that police boards appear to play almost no helpful role in clarifying issues important to policing.

The ability of a board to avoid its job can be seen at virtually any meeting. In the case of the Board of

Commissioners of Police of Metro Toronto, the main agenda item is usually the awarding of citations to officers or citizens for acts of bravery, heroism or neighbourliness. Such events are held mostly for the purpose of attracting media attention. These presentations are usually followed by the board's consideration of tenders, promotions and other detailed matters of administration, none of which are particularly debatable. Then, in speedy fashion, the board adjourns.

On some occasions public deputations are made to the board, in which case the board will listen politely, then refer the matter to staff for comment. Some weeks later the matter will be back on the board's agenda in a form it can file away. The board goes to great pains to avoid any public debate of any substantive policing matters. Such debate may take place in private, but there are few signs that it does. It seems that the other boards in other jurisdictions act in a similar fashion.

As debate on policing has increased in the last decade, the vacuum of police governance has been questioned on four fronts:

Public Accountability

There are two divergent views on the extent of public accountability of police governing bodies. Prime Minister Trudeau outlined one view while commenting on the RCMP in 1977:

> The policy of this government...has been that they indeed — the politicians who happen to form the government — should be kept in ignorance of the day to day operations of the police force and even the security force....That is our position. It is not one of pleading ignorance to defend the government. It is one of keeping the government's nose out of the oper-

LOCAL POLICE GOVERNANCE IN CANADA, U.S.A. AND U.K.

	Ontario		British Columbia	Alberta
	Forces in Small Municipalities	Forces in Regions and Municipalities of More than 15,000		
Local Police Authority	Council or board	Board	Board	Board
Membership on Local Authority	3 if board, majority by province	5 in regions; 3 in cities. Majority by province	5: mayor, 1 councillor, 3 by province	All appointed by council (some not from council)
Budget Approval	Council (or board if there is one)	Board (ratified by council)	Board (ratified by council)	Council
Appointment of Chief	Council (or board if there is one)	Board	Board	Board
Grant for Police Purposes and Other Government Levels	$10/capita, but unconditional to council	$15/capita in regions, $10/capita in cities, towns, but unconditional to council	No	Portion of unconditional grant
% of Police Budget Locally Raised	50%–70%	66%–80%	100%	80%

LOCAL POLICE GOVERNANCE IN CANADA, U.S.A. AND U.K. (cont.)

	Quebec	Nova Scotia	Typical U.S. City	U.S. Variant	United Kingdom
Local Police Authority	Council (except Montreal & Quebec)	Board	Council	Council	Watch Committee of council
Membership on Local Authority	No board (except as above)	All appointed by council (some not from council)	No board	No board	Majority from council; minority are local magistrates
Budget Approval	Council	Council	Council	Council	Council
Appointment of Chief	Mayor (except as above)	Council	Mayor	City manager (sometimes State Civil Service Procedures)	Local Watch Committee but from Home Office List
Grant for Police Purposes and Other Government Levels	Yes	Yes	State grants rare. Special Federal Law Enforcement assistance and some unconditional revenue sharing	Some states have police grants	50% matching grant—most expenses eligible
% of Police Budget Locally Raised	75%–80%	Varies and increasing rapidly	95%–100%	As low as 60% in some California cities	40%–50%

Source: Provincial and State Municipal Affairs Departments. August. 1978. For United Kingdom. various secondary sources.

ation of the police force, at whatever level of government. On the criminal law side, the protections we
have against abuse are not with the government, they
are with the courts.[23]

Other advocates of this view embrace the idea of
having an appointed board — rather than politicians
— govern the police, but still declare that policing is
too crucial to security to be exposed to the comment
and controversy that will attend any public discussion.
The opposing view to Trudeau's was put equally
forcefully by K.C. Palmer in his 1979 study:

> The arguments for "keeping politics out of the police"
> are largely fraudulent. No matter how the system is
> structured, the police governing body must ultimately
> be responsible to the public — that is accountability
> and that is politics. The present system where the
> provincial government, elected through a party system,
> appoints a majority of police commissioners is every
> bit as "political" and more potentially dangerous than
> a situation in which a government composed of twenty-
> four separately elected individuals [on the Kitchener-
> Waterloo Council] with at least three different political
> stripes and seven different factions appoints a police
> governing body.[24]

Some say that policing is too important *not* to be
done in full view of the public. They argue that budgets
should be more detailed and more accessible; meetings
should be more public, without the board continually
reverting to private session. The commission should
not discuss specific cases in public any more than city
officials should publicly discuss whether a certain citizen has paid his taxes and water bill. But the commission should lift the veil on the broad direction of
policies.

The Size of Police Boards

In Ontario there has been widespread discussion for several years about the best size of a police board. At the present time, police boards in regional municipalities have a membership of five; those in smaller municipalities, three. A number of arguments have been made in support of a larger board. First, a larger board provides more opportunities for representation of minorities, an important consideration in cities where there is an ethnic mix. Suggestions have been made that a board of seven, nine or even eleven would be more appropriate.

As well, a small board works against any notion of community discussion being reflected in the board's deliberations. If the board is small, then there simply won't be enough people to foster discussion, nor to carry on divisive and complex debates. In the same way, it is argued that a larger board will be better able to raise issues that are then discussed publicly, rather than simply responding to debate begun by others, and that it will have the manpower to consult with the public in formal and informal ways.

The Composition of Police Boards

The two questions here are who chooses the members of police boards and how many of the members should be elected politicians. Canadian cities show the great range of options available. A preponderance of politicians suggests that police should be controlled by elected officials; a dearth, that the interests of politicians are too narrow, too short-term to be helpful. Further, some suggest that elected politicians will not have the time to spend on policing that might be available to an appointed citizen without other public tasks.

This argument devolves into one about the ability of electoral politics to grapple with public issues, an issue much larger than the scope of this book.

A question related to the size of elected representation is whether the police governing body should be a direct arm of the local council, as opposed to a provincially controlled body. Municipal government in Canada has considerable experience with special purpose bodies set up to administer a specific local function — boards for parks, libraries, arenas, community centres, as well as parking authorities and historical boards. The idea of a police board is well within this municipal tradition, whether or not it is seen as desirable for the policing function.

In most jurisdictions other than Ontario, the local council has the power to appoint a majority of the police board, thus ensuring that police are under local control. Majority appointment by provincial rather than local authorities in Ontario has caused considerable tension in that province, leading to the charge that the province, which pays less than 20 per cent of local policing costs in larger centres, has retained its appointment powers to ensure that police are not responsible to local authorities in theory or in practice.

Kinds of Tenure

Lengthy tenure can ensure that board members have a thorough knowledge of policing operations, but it can also mean that any member who is simply not willing to take the job of helpful critic seriously can coast through the years. Shorter tenure can result in constant infusions of new energy and insights, but can equally lead to a lack of long-term planning, timidity on the part of the appointee, and an unknowledgeable board. This is a conundrum faced in all areas of public service.

In a similar vein, a part-time appointee may be more willing to accept the advice of senior staff without question than someone who has the time and energy to do independent research and make his own connections within the organization. Some kind of balance is required to ensure that appointees do not try to involve themselves with day-to-day management — that must be left to senior police officials — but have a firm grasp of what the organization is doing and where it is headed.

Are Police Boards Helpful?

Of course, the central question is whether police boards are effective at all. Often boards have functioned as a buffer between the police and the public rather than as a means of communicating. They have been considered bodies that isolate rather than integrate; they shield and shelter police practices rather than explain and improve them.

These criticisms have not led to wholesale changes. Instead, the criticisms have been countered with the evocation of fears of introducing a state of affairs similar to that in many American police departments. It is frequently suggested that political intervention in Canadian policing will result in the corruption and deviance found in American forces. This criticism is unfair, as it conveniently forgets the traditions of municipal government in Canada.

In American cities one of the perquisites of a mayor's power is that he or she gets to appoint all senior officials — the city treasurer, the chief planner and the heads of all departments, including the police chief.

Thus, the head of the police is a political appointee and can be expected to shape the police department in ways that the mayor will see appropriate. There is some question whether Lord Denning's dicta concerning political direction given to the police chief are entirely applicable to American police forces, given the closer relationship between the politicians and senior officers.

Such arrangements do not exist in Canadian cities. Mayors in Canada do not get to appoint any civil servants. Canadian cities follow the British model of an independent civil service that is there to serve the government of the day. In return, it is expected that the civil service will not be tampered with. Policing services are viewed in the same way. The kinds of political interference experienced in American police departments are simply not found in Canada — this holds no matter how many elected politicians are on the local police board.

The questions posed in this chapter strike at the heart of police relations with society at large. Fear of crime has so blinded the public that questions of the role of police are rarely touched on, leaving police organizations to determine their own relevance. The fallout that comes from not confronting these questions creates problems for individual officers, problems that are discussed in the next chapter.

5
Police Politics and Personality

Why do police officers all seem so similar?

There are two contrasting views about why certain human traits fit certain jobs. Either the applicant gets hired because he has the right traits or the job moulds the person, so their character conforms.

In the case of the police, we've seen how strict entrance standards mean that people with personalities considered inappropriate by the recruiting officers are weeded out at the start. Further, because of their unique management practices, there is a powerful tendency within police forces for officers to band together and reinforce each other's personality. The selection mechanisms and job pressures combine to produce a fairly coherent police personality.

There are two key variables to police work. One is danger. More than most other members of society, police voluntarily enter dangerous situations. Although not frequent, these incidents can erupt without warning from the most innocent-looking circumstances. The danger could result from simply stopping a car for a traffic violation; a gun is pulled and the car speeds away. It could arise when an officer responds to a domestic dispute or arrives at the scene of a fire. These situations are as familiar as the daily news.

The second variable is authority. The officer is constantly expected to respond with an aura of authority, to bring order to a situation in disarray, to take control in the face of threatening, deviant behaviour. The police become involved in disputes that others can't resolve. In fact, the very solution is often simply that the police take control. Society's response to a situation of danger is the imposition of authority.

These two variables, danger and authority, will be discussed in regard to their effects on the individual officer, on policing as an occupation, and on the public perception of police activities.[1]

Danger

The first reaction to danger is suspicion. To perform well, perhaps even to survive, an officer must always be on the lookout for what might happen next. This constant state of aroused suspicion leads to cynicism and an expectation of the worst from people.

The public interprets this cynicism as police putting themselves at a distance, as though the police are not part of the normal social order; over time two camps emerge — police and others. Indeed, as we've seen, this division is deepened by the deliberate segregation begun with police recruitment and then training. Even at a social function such as a party the presence of an off-duty police officer causes unease.

Being required on a daily basis to face the possibility of danger leads the officer to seek the orderly, the predictable. Orderly situations are quickly read and any dangers easy to identify. Over the years the officer can be expected to see plenty of good in a conservative society where people know their place and do not try to push for speedy change. As an organization, police can be expected to resist experimentation on either the individual or societal level.

Accordingly, the public perception is that the police are a conservative group and not quite "up with the times." This perception is enhanced by the distinct uniforms officers wear in contrast to the varying sartorial styles of politicians and professionals who have abandoned practical dress. The same is true of hairstyles.

Danger also isolates the officer. The public may run from situations of danger, but the police officer has a duty to stay. This solitary position, experienced in the physical world, is reflected in social relations.

As a group, the police interpret this isolation as a signal that the protection of society is up to them and no one else. They feel they are "the blue wall," protecting the rest of us; if they can't do the job, no one will. In dangerous situations, police may well conclude, "It's up to us, we should do what we think appropriate." In turn, the public concludes that the police are "a law unto themselves." They do what has to be done, and they don't seem too concerned with dissenters who would urge caution. Clearly this is a double standard created by the public: to first abandon situations to the police and then complain that police do what they want. But this *is* a fair assessment of the dynamics.

Apart from its isolating effect, living in a constant state of imagined danger is not conducive to personal puritanism. It is much like being in a low-level war where little apart from the safety of oneself and one's colleagues seems of importance. In this state the bounds of acceptable behaviour appear to be freer.

Many officers respond just as other people in this situation do — with lax personal standards. There are frequent reports that groups of police officers hold stags with strippers and various lewd performances, often accompanied by heavy drinking. To the public these pastimes appear hypocritical, since these are the very officers who should be upholding public morals, the very officers who charge others for sexual and alcohol-related offences.

Authority

The exercise of authority also isolates, and to some extent results in social ostracism. The ultimate example is the prime minister, whose life is considerably less free than others in society, given the kinds of protection needed to keep him both from an admiring (or hostile) public and from those who wish to attack authority directly. To a lesser extent, the same ostracism is felt by police officers. Police are called upon to bring order to unbalanced situations, and this exercise of authority isolates them just as much as confronting danger does. Police are led to believe that they are different from others in society not only because they are willing to face up to problems others shy away from, but because they possess an important social privilege not available to others.

This exercise of authority deepens the occupational solidarity so noticeable in police officers. Their elite position is driven home in the emotionally powerful display of gathering for the funeral of a colleague killed in the line of duty. The gathering itself is a sign that police are the social and moral authority that was pierced in the officer's death, but not broken.

In exercising authority, police are upholding the rules made by those in power and thus supporting directly those who make the rules. Just as with danger, authority drives the police to keep things the way they are, and to discourage those who would experiment with social norms. That is the nature of acting on behalf of authority.

This characteristic pervades every police force. It leads police to believe that their job is to enforce all the laws all the time, a claim that senior officers make to justify many questionable police actions. The public sees this behaviour as hypocritical, since laws are clearly enforced on a discretionary basis.

In fact, anyone enforcing rules on a daily basis can quickly become authoritarian and believe in authority as an end in itself deserving respect and obedience. It is easy to become intolerant of the deviant, of those who won't stay in line. This intolerance is most often exhibited by the police against minorities who wish to do things a bit differently from the norm. Most minorities feel that police do discriminate against them.[2]

The worst part of trying to enforce rules is the resentment from those who want to go their own way. Any rule enforcer is bound to be disliked, to be resented, to be joked about. The police officer senses these attitudes on a continuing basis, and his response is often the assertion of authority in as strong a method as possible. To show who is in control in any situation, however calm, police might resort to violence and intimidation.

Trying to explain this violence in terms of the ''bad apple'' misses the point: given what the police are expected to do, violence is bound to occur as they fulfil the role they think the public assigns them.

The above analysis is a speculative description of police characteristics, specifically the effect of the dominant conditions — danger and authority — on officers. Not all officers will be affected to the same degree by these pressures, but the pressures are nevertheless there. The most well-adjusted officer is bound to act in the ways described, despite personal reservations, simply because the job demands it. No changes to recruitment techniques or standards will alter these influences. The main determinants of the police personality are structural in nature.

These problems are exacerbated through the recruitment process, since that process is staffed by those who have already adapted to the pressures of the job. They know the applicants whose character will fit police work, as well as those who will fall by the wayside. Thus, the police personality is reinforced at the entry point.

A more traditional analysis of the police character concludes that the actual tasks performed, and the people the police are in constant contact with, are the determining factors. Police deal with the crooked, the weak, the unscrupulous. A driver stopped for a traffic violation can often become abusive or give a false excuse. Drunks are malicious, violent, insulting and frequently revolting. Quarrelling spouses turn on the police who are seen as intruders in a private dispute.

These experiences are not pleasant and can often lead an officer to become cynical about human nature. He is driven to assume that human motives are of the lowest order. None of this kind of work increases self-esteem or self-respect, nor does it lead one to believe that the world might become a better place.

The American criminologist Alfred Neiderhoffer, himself a former police officer, argues that the pessimism flowing from the attempt to enforce laws leads to such low self-esteem that officers suffer from anomie — a loss of faith in people — and a loss of enthusiasm for high ideals. Anomie results in a lack of pride and integrity, and the feeling that self-expression is difficult, leading to withdrawal.

For the police officer, one of the few rewards of work is catching a criminal and ensuring he is punished. The rest of the time, officers retreat into secrecy and clubism in order to support each other in an essentially unpleasant world. The shared job experience enhances the social ostracism of police. For this reason police associations are quite strong, not only in their dealings with police authorities, but as a force in society generally.

Deviance

Distinctions must be made between various kinds of police wrongdoing. When an officer acts for his own personal gain or satisfaction, such as pocketing money found during a search, it is referred to as misbehaviour. This kind of individual deviance can occur in any bureaucracy, and nothing further need be said about it here.

Corruption occurs when police as a group act for their own personal gain or satisfaction. Such cases usually involve informal rules set by officers about how certain incidents will be handled, and the amounts of money that each will receive for the part played. This will be discussed later in the chapter.

A third kind of wrongdoing involves systematically bending the rules to produce a certain outcome, not for personal gain or satisfaction, but because the result is considered desirable within the force. This is "police deviance." The officers receive no personal benefits other than job satisfaction and the support of colleagues. Some critics suggest that the exercise of discretion is little more than a justification for deviant behaviour: "Much of the literature on police discretion...can in fact be viewed as an analysis of structured organizational deviance."[3]

One example of police deviance is the treatment of persons under arrest. As we saw earlier, "many more people are detained prior to trial than are jailed after sentence."[4] This is directly contrary to notions about being innocent until proven guilty, since it shows that the police are harsher in "sentencing" thus-far innocent suspects than judges are with convicted criminals. Police have a practice of twisting rules regarding arrest and incarceration to achieve the results they want.

The Bail Reform Act states that an accused has the right not to be held in custody for most offences unless the arresting officer has reasonable and probable grounds to believe either that the accused will fail to attend trial or that the release of the person poses a threat to the public interest. These tests give the officer plenty of latitude in deciding whether the accused should remain in custody. Research shows that the likelihood of being convicted is substantially increased if there is a pre-trial detention: in this way an officer's decision on incarceration will have an effect on the final outcome of the case.[5]

In making a decision about incarceration, the officer takes into account such factors as the suspect's marital status, employment status (i.e., the unemployed are less responsible, and more likely to skip the trial), and the extent to which he or she has cooperated. Yet studies show that the unemployed are more likely to attend trial than the employed. And surely the reforms in the Bail Reform Act were never meant not to apply to a suspect who felt no obligation to cooperate with the police. The police have managed to skew the law in ways that produce the results they want, namely, a relatively certain conviction against certain kinds of individuals. This kind of deviant behaviour has important consequences for suspects but is not particularly visible to the public.[6]

A different example of deviant behaviour can emerge when officers are required to give testimony in respect to possible wrongdoings by their comrades. In a 1984 case before Toronto's Police Complaints Board regarding the police assault on one David Footman on the street and later in a police garage, the board began its brief decision with these remarkable paragraphs:

> Before dealing with the charges, we feel it is important that we have serious concerns about the reliability of the evidence of several of the police witnesses who gave evidence in this hearing. We will mention three specific instances. Firstly, all of the officers who gave evidence about events at the scene were unable to identify any of their colleagues who had discussions with the civilians. These same officers were able to identify colleagues in cars at a distance. One cannot help but draw the conclusion that these officers were acting to protect themselves or their fellow officers.
>
> Secondly, the evidence of P.C. Colmanero and Horwood was virtually identical in those items they were able to remember and those details they were unable to recall. We were left with the impression that they had agreed upon their evidence in advance.
>
> Thirdly, and most particularly, the unique ability of the four officers that testified about the events in the garage at 11 Division to recall the specific details of those events, as compared to their inability to recall other and more significant events challenges their credibility. This is not the first time that this concern about police organizing their testimony has been raised and in the long-run it will reduce the value of police testimony.[7]

According to the board, the police were bending their evidence in a traditional police cause, namely, protecting each other in their work.

A more visible kind of deviance occurs when the police break the law "in a good cause," as in the cases of the raids on gay bathhouses in Toronto mentioned earlier and the RCMP's "dirty tricks" campaign against the Quebec nationalist movement, which we will return to later in this chapter.

Some have suggested that police leave toy guns in the vicinity of persons killed by police bullets in order to justify their action. Many people think the police have a habit of beating up teenagers on a regular basis.

Deviancy is supported by the police subculture and by the public's hesitance to question police actions, so that focusing public attention on deviance is difficult. Often acts that are deviant in nature are explained as the work of a "bad apple" — though the incident complained of is just one that happens to have emerged from a larger pattern.

Indeed, almost all police wrongdoing is dismissed by police authorities as individual misbehaviour, and charges are laid under the Police Act against the offending officer. If wrongdoing is seen in this light, then structural changes are not required, nor are policy directives, since every organization, even the police, can count on having its misfits. But if the acts *are* deviant — part of widely accepted police behaviour — this explanation is unsatisfactory, and the usual remedies, focused on cautioning the individual, will not be sufficient.

Corruption

Police corruption — where police act in concert for personal gain — appears not to be widespread in

Canada. There are few examples that can be pointed to. In the United States, on the other hand, there are countless examples of corrupt behaviour, and many police forces in large cities have been infected. Examples of what American police are willing to do in return for money are almost without limit: agreeing not to arrest or prosecute those known to have broken the law; agreeing to drop an investigation prematurely by not pursuing promising leads; reducing charges; changing testimony; altering police records; converting seized goods (such as drugs) for personal use.[8] In New York, police have been caught taking payments from construction firms for the right to back cement trucks over the sidewalks to reach construction sites. Given the latitude of police discretion and the great number of laws that might be enforced, the opportunities for officers to devise ways to charge a personal licence fee are almost infinite.

Police corruption has a substantial impact. First, it reduces respect for the law. Second, officers preoccupied with carrying out and worrying about their corrupt activities may do little policing, and certainly would have little energy left to care about, say, individual or minority rights. Finally, in cities where police corruption is rampant, others in the criminal justice system are usually also tainted by corruption. If the officer sees that judges, lawyers and politicians are all on the take, it is quite within the realm of reason for him to conclude that he might as well be part of the action.

Once entrenched, corruption is difficult to battle. First, where should the line be drawn? Should an officer accept a free cup of coffee? At the same restaurant every day, or once a week? A free sandwich, or lunch, or dinner? What of the businessman on the beat who

can get a good deal on a TV set? A freezer? A swimming pool? At what point is the officer compromised
by gifts? When the gift is a furniture suite? A mort-
gage?

Most Canadian forces draw the line right at the top:
officers can accept nothing.[9] An absolute rule can often
be waived for minor gifts like coffee, but can be effectively called on when police accept more. At that point,
senior officers can be sent in to levy appropriate discipline.

But once corruption has eaten into a force, it is
difficult to secure incriminating evidence against officers. There is a natural conspiracy of silence where
officers refuse to speak out against one another. Those
outside corrupt circles will be leery of tattling on their
colleagues, while those on the take have good reason
not to speak, as movies such as *Serpico* and *Prince of
the City* — both based on real episodes in New York
City — show. To be effective, attacks on police
corruption must be done publicly and quickly, and they
must be tough and fair. Making an accusation that
cannot be substantiated destroys valid arguments, and
dragging out accusations only gives the opportunity
for those involved to destroy evidence or create alibis.

Those who wish to expose corruption must provide
a forum and a safe place for officers who want to tell
what they know and be protected from unpleasant and
perhaps deadly consequences. In the United States,
independent commissions have been found to be the
most successful tool for these purposes. Trying to fight
corruption from within seems difficult. Reorganizing
the force in order to break up corrupt groups works
only with a force that is slightly infected.

Dealing with Police Wrongdoing

All police forces receive complaints about police wrongdoing, and requests for apologies or other rectification. The number of complaints varies widely. Calgary, with a force of 1,085 uniformed officers policing a community of 385,000, received 44 complaints in 1980, of which 27 related to the use of excessive force. Winnipeg, with a force of 1,007 uniformed officers policing 600,000 residents, received 174 complaints in 1979, of which 47 related to the use of excessive force.

Most Canadian forces have a special division that receives and investigates complaints, and then reports both to the chief and to the complainant. Most complaints are judged to be unfounded. In the Calgary example, 12 were sustained in whole or in part; in Winnipeg, 53 were sustained. The discipline imposed on officers as a result is not known. Suggestions that self-investigation is too biased to produce helpful results are met with the retort that police are professional enough to review complaints seriously, and in any case it is in the interest of the police force to rid itself of the legendary "bad apples."

Complainants who are not satisfied with the response to their complaint have other options open to them. If the complaint involves violence — often people complain that police assault them, push them down stairs or use other methods of coercion — then a charge can be laid before a justice of the peace. However, there are significant problems with this procedure. First, if the charge is accepted by the justice of the peace, then prosecution is passed to the crown attorney, and control of the matter is lost by the complainant. Crown attorneys spend almost all their time in court prosecuting for the police, and it is difficult for them to turn on the police and seek a conviction. Complainants who lay charges are often dissatisfied with the manner in which cases are handled by crown attorneys.

Second, chances for the complainant in the courtroom are poor, even when the crown attorney handles the prosecution well. In many instances where police violence is alleged, the event occurred when the complainant was alone, without independent witnesses. The case turns on the complainant's word versus that of the officer and his partner. In this situation a judge will most often believe the officers rather than the complainant. On the balance of evidence, it is most unlikely the complaint will be confirmed.

Third, the consequences of not making the charge stick can be severe. For many years in Toronto the police force had the habit of laying malicious prosecution charges against the complainants who had been unsuccessful in court. The complainant might find that as well as having to pay his lawyer's expenses, *he* is convicted of a criminal offence rather than the officer who caused the problem in the first place. The police officer does not run this risk; traditionally, the force covers the cost of defending the officer in criminal trials and of pursuing malicious prosecution cases.

Because of these problems, complainants are well advised not to lay criminal charges.

Another course of action is to appeal to the police commission. One can argue that the complaint was not investigated fairly or thoroughly, and that the case should be reviewed. This approach has rarely been helpful. The processing of complaints does not often involve a paper trail or written summary of who was interviewed and what was said, making it difficult to allege that the investigation was improper. There is no record on which the complainant can rely in approaching the governing authority, and thus its members will be most loath to conclude that their subordinates have acted improperly.

Many jurisdictions permit the complainant a public hearing before the police governing authority, as though this constitutes a reasonable way to handle complaints. In any event, few hearings are held, and appeals made to provincial police authorities in Ontario, British Columbia or Quebec are even rarer.

Civil action can also be pursued. This route is costly, lengthy and chancy: rarely could one expect a financial award against an officer when the complaints division of the police force has not sustained the complaint. The complainant can appeal to the media, but the best the publicity can lead to is a further internal investigation by police authorities, with all of the problems mentioned above.

Last, if an allegation can be made that the injustice suffered is one of a pattern of similar events, one can urge the establishment of a royal commission to investigate. This is such a spectacular solution that it is rarely invoked and then only on the basis of a string of publicized complaints. In any case, once a commission is established, the complainant loses all control of his case.

Many have expressed dissatisfaction with these methods of dealing with grievances. Given their power, it has often been argued that having police investigate themselves is simply not good enough; complaints should be reviewed independently. The most widely publicized call for an independent complaint process was made by criminal lawyer Arthur Maloney, who was retained in 1975 by the Metro Toronto Police Commission to report on the problem of complaints.

His recommendation was not adopted. In a 1978 study by Walter Pitman for the Metro Toronto government on police/minority relations, the same recommendation was made. Finally, in 1980 the Ontario government introduced legislation permitting a three-year experiment with a new complaints mechanism in Toronto.

The legislation flowed from a study done for the province by Sydney Linden, a noted civil rights lawyer. Linden examined approaches to police complaints in American and European cities, and concluded that a totally independent body would not succeed. He thought police would stymie independent investigation with a wall of silence.

Linden proposed that the police be involved in the investigation of the complaint, and that the results of the investigation be in writing and be reported to the complainant, the police and an independent board set up to review complaints and their investigation. It was a hybrid proposal constructed to retain the confidence of the police and to attract the confidence of the public. The proposal became law in 1981, and Linden was appointed the first public complaints commissioner.

The Office of the Public Complaints Commission consists of a staff of investigators, clerks and lawyers. It is headed by a board of twenty-four civilians, appointed in equal numbers by Metro Toronto Council, the Metro Toronto Police Association, and the provincial cabinet. The function of the board is to hear cases where a complainant is unsatisfied with the investigation and its outcome. The general procedure is as follows:

(i)   A complaint is filed with the police or with the Public Complaints Office.

(ii) Police begin their investigation, and must report within thirty days to the commission and to the complainant on the course of investigation. The report must be in writing, stating who the police investigators have talked to and what evidence they have gathered. If the investigation is not completed, then the report summarizes the state of affairs. If it is completed, the complainant is told of the disposition of the matter.

Police investigators do not settle complaints. Their job is to gather evidence, and a senior police officer independent of the investigation decides on the basis of the evidence what should be done. Thus, there is some attempt to separate out the fact-finding function from the judgmental function.

In unusual cases, the commission is permitted to intervene directly before the expiry of thirty days after the complaint is filed. After the first thirty days, the commission is permitted as of right to intervene in the investigation. If it appears that police investigators are not proceeding expeditiously, the commission can begin its own investigation.

(iii) If the complainant is unhappy about the disposition of the complaint, he may ask the complaints commissioner to review the matter. The commissioner may obtain his own information and can interview any appropriate parties. The commissioner may make his own findings about what happened.

(iv) If the complainant remains unsatisfied, the commissioner can be asked to order a hearing before a panel selected from the twenty-four-member board. All parties can be represented by legal counsel, and can call evidence they think appropriate.

In 1983, 758 complaints were filed with the Public Complaints Office, over half of which alleged police assault. Of all cases, no action was taken on 314 because of insufficient evidence; in 48 cases the police version was corroborated by independent witnesses; and 102 cases were withdrawn. A further 214 cases were resolved informally, with the officer and the complainant reaching some agreeable middle ground through apologies and explanations on both sides. In 45 cases the officer was deemed to have acted legally. That leaves the 34 cases where disciplinary action was taken: 22 officers were cautioned or counselled; 9 were charged under the Police Act; and 3 were charged under the Criminal Code.[10]

In all, the Public Complaints Board completed six hearings in 1983, and five more were scheduled or in process. Of those completed, the board found there was insufficient evidence to sustain the complaints in three cases, and in the other three the complaints were upheld and penalties imposed.

There is no question but that this system is a substantial improvement over other complaint mechanisms in Canada. It requires that police investigators report in detail about the investigation, thus throwing public light on a process that was previously private. It requires that reports are in writing so there is a continuing record of how the complaint is being dealt with. It permits independent review of both the investigation and the conclusions drawn from the evidence. Many argue that these improvements are a useful counterbalance to the fact that police themselves still undertake investigation in the first thirty days.

Yet there are strong criticisms by both the Canadian Civil Liberties Association and the Citizens Independent Review of Police Actions (CIRPA) that this process has not gone far enough. Both groups say that public perception is a crucial issue: people won't complain if they feel the complaint won't be dealt with fairly. Since the investigation continues to be done by police, many people will continue to think their complaint will come to naught. Some critics argue that giving police the first thirty days to investigate allows them ample opportunity to protect themselves and perhaps even destroy incriminating evidence. Thus, the suspicion that police are covering up for their peers is not removed by the Public Complaints Commission, and perhaps constitutes a serious drawback.

A further criticism is that misconduct can only be established under this process if the officer is found guilty beyond a reasonable doubt, the same burden of proof as in a criminal trial. It is a burden of proof so high that it will rarely be met. An early criticism was that one-third of the members of the board were appointed by the Police Association — which has a very special interest in what happens to officers — but this was blunted by the quality of those appointments.

The Public Complaints Commission has been accepted by the police community in spite of its requirements for substantially more disclosure than heretofore demanded of any Canadian police force. It is a giant step away from the informality with which complaints were previously processed. In late 1984, legislation was passed removing the commission from an experimental status and confirming it as permanent.

This complaint mechanism continues to deal with complaints on a one-by-one basis. Police deviance is not on the agenda, nor is any behaviour that derives from police structures. Wrongdoing is still seen to spring from an officer who has acted in an aberrant fashion.

Dirty Tricks

One severe form of police deviance has become widely known and is referred to as dirty tricks. These tricks consist of police actions taken ''in a good cause,'' where police perform acts that are clearly criminal in nature, done with intent, but according to police done in the interests of society as a whole.

Most dirty tricks are around questions of national security, where the villains are those said to be trying to destroy the state or foment radical political change. This distinguishes these actions from other forms of deviance, such as harassing homosexuals, youths or other minorities, vulnerable because the police can count on many in society to support such actions out of prejudice. Dirty tricks are aimed at those who, in the opinion of police officials, wish to overthrow society and take away traditional liberties.

Dirty tricks came to the fore in Canada in the 1970s, with the main theatre of operations being Quebec. Two royal commissions have been held into these kinds of activities: the Keable Commission in Quebec, and the McDonald Commission of Inquiry Concerning Certain Activities of the RCMP at the federal level. A third inquiry, the Laycraft Commission in Alberta, looked at other illegal police activities, specifically wiretapping. The dirty tricks that have become public have all been carried out by the national police force, and to that extent are somewhat outside the scope of this book. Accordingly, they will be touched on only briefly.

Operation Bricole involved the October 1972 break-in by RCMP officers Robert Samson and Claude Brodeur at the shared offices of a separatist news agency, L'Agence Presse Libre du Québec (APLQ), and the Movement for the Defence of Political Prisoners of Quebec. The RCMP had the support and cooperation of the head of the Montreal police intelligence department, although not of the force as a whole. Aside from breaking into the APLQ offices without a warrant, the operation included the theft of many boxes of material — in fact, so much material that it could not be stored and sifted in Montreal Police headquarters. Instead it was kept in Claude Brodeur's basement. Although the APLQ sent letters to numerous politicians claiming that the police were responsible for the break-in, there was a successful cover-up of police involvement for more than three years. An investigation by the Montreal police force into the break-in was stymied by the RCMP.

As a senior RCMP officer said to the McDonald Commission, in the Security Service "we accept some things as routine to the point that we don't think of them as illegal....In the security field laws seem less important than in the criminal field. This is a myth, of course, but it is accepted....We should, if possible, act within the law. But if the law doesn't permit us to take the necessary steps we consider violating [it]...."[11]

Other dirty tricks were performed by the RCMP Security Service in the early 1970s, including the burning of a barn, the stealing of dynamite and blasting caps, and the issuance of a fake terrorist communiqué. As author Jeff Sallot notes, "All this was done in the name of national security."[12]

The RCMP routinely opened and tampered with mail at least since the mid-Fifties, eventually under the code name of Operation Cathedral. This practice was directed against those thought to be national security risks. Operation Ham involved a break-in to obtain the computer tapes of the Parti Québécois membership, an organization that was certainly not illegal or underground, yet one that the Security Service must have seen as a threat to the national interest.[13]

It is fair to conclude that the police — at least from the examples of the RCMP just cited — have a political agenda of their own. They form decisions about the kinds of problems they think the Canadian state faces, and then devise methods to act on those decisions. Obviously, they feel they have both the power and the authority to act on their beliefs, and do so — and this is perhaps confirmed by the fact that the officers committing criminal acts have either not been prosecuted or, when prosecuted, have been given absolute discharges. The police know that they have a relatively free hand in these matters. Chances are they will not be caught out in their dirty tricks, and if they are, they will not face censure or any other penalty.

At the municipal level it is entirely possible that intelligence divisions are also involved in dirty tricks that relate not to national security, but instead to perceptions police have about who constitutes a threat to urban stability. In Kitchener, police authorities forced members of motorcycle gangs to kneel down in the station and follow orders, to show obeisance. In Niagara Falls, police performed body searches on young women who frequented an establishment said to be a centre for drugs. Many political activists think police infiltrate all kinds of protest groups in order both to gain intelligence and to influence group activities. Perhaps police think their political agenda entitles them to protect their idea of the public good at whatever cost, a sentiment certainly derived from the police personality and understandable in terms of the public's expectations.

Police Politics

As illustrated in chapter 3, police associations are powerful organizations, often exerting considerable influence over the way in which policing operations are carried out. They also play a political role in the life of the community. That role has a number of aspects. Boxing clubs are run by individual officers with substantial support by the police hierarchy. Police cars often sport bumper stickers for various charities — one of the few groups of civil servants expected to show open support in this way. Police associations stage large sporting competitions, usually choosing a beauty queen. One might consider these kinds of activities as passively political, since the political message given is the demonstration of concern for society's well-being.

The police chief is expected to play a prominent role in the community. The chief is a welcome guest at banquets and some political events, and is given a seat of honour. He is often quoted about community matters, and his opinion is given great weight.

A more explicitly political role for the police is involvement in legislative change. During the redrafting of Ontario's Police Act during 1983 and 1984, police associations were involved in all of the private (and secret) meetings with elected officials from the municipal and provincial levels as the terms of the legislation were hammered out. No other groups were allowed to find out exactly what was going on. The police enjoyed a political status denied to others. When the Toronto Public Complaints Commission, just discussed, was being put in place, three bodies were permitted to make appointments to it: Metro Council, the provincial cabinet and the Police Association. The association said it would attempt to scupper the attempted reforms to complaint procedures if it didn't get its share of the appointments.

Police associations have also been overtly political when they deem it in their self-interest. This can take the form of working for something, such as a return to capital punishment, or against something, like a contrary politician. When New York Mayor John Lindsay attempted to establish a citizens complaint board in the late 1960s, police worked against him and ensured his defeat at the polls.*

---

* My own experience is relevant to this discussion. When I was running for re-election as mayor of Toronto in 1980, police campaigned actively against me. According to press reports, leaders of the police association were taking up a collection within the force for this purpose. Further, signs were placed in police station locker rooms advising officers to "flush Sewell down the drain," among other things, and pamphlets excoriating homosexuals (I had spoken up for them) were distributed from police stations. While the chief at one point requested officers to remove the signs in the locker rooms, there was no public apology, no attempt to rein in this activity. My election workers worried what effect "Support Sewell" buttons would have for those wearing them if stopped by police officers, and there was some reluctance to wear them. The effect of the police action was not at all subtle and probably quite effective in showing that police found me an unacceptable candidate. Since I lost that election by less than 2,000 votes (about 1 per cent of all votes cast), it is fair to say that police action probably had some effect on that election. There was no public outcry about this behaviour. It was as though political action by police was expected and considered legitimate.

This kind of collective political activity by police raises two concerns. First, there is a long-standing tradition in Canada that civil servants may not participate collectively in political affairs. In some provinces, this tradition has been embodied in legislation. Political involvement by individuals is considered acceptable, but there is a line that is crossed when civil servants attempt to have a collective influence on their masters. Police appear to breach this line without censure.

Second, it is important that there be a distinction between those who make the laws and those who enforce them. This is especially the case in respect to criminal law, where the ramifications are so severe and where rights can be so easily affected. Police should not be judge and jury; yet if they succeed in both making and enforcing laws, they become a law unto themselves and the public has no one to turn to for protection.

Given society's uneasiness with criticism of the police, these issues have not received substantial debate in Canadian cities. Yet the concerns are clear. Police political activity is going one better than a dirty trick.

Deviance, corruption and dirty tricks are the main fodder of public discussion about policing. Occasional references are made in the media to the police personality but rarely in terms that give a context to that personality or to its collective expression, police unionism. It is clear that the larger questions of crime, police objectives and social expectations bear on the police personality, and officers will not be free of the burdens those questions impose until there is a much fuller understanding of the nature of policing. The kinds of reforms that would be helpful in that regard are discussed in the next chapter.

6
Reforming the Police

As noted in chapter 4, society has been unclear about the nature of the police function. While legislative duties hardly go beyond a crime fighting role, that duty takes up only a small percentage of police time. A helpful start would be a wide-ranging agreement on police goals and objectives.

Comparing North American police practices with those of other cultures helps provide a perspective on the problem.[1] Japan, for example, provides an interesting contrast. There, police stations are simply fixed police posts, called *kobans*. The typical *koban* is a small office on the street (in some instances attached to the officer's residence) that serves a population of just over 10,000. It is a general one-stop help centre for the community, of particular service in Tokyo to those looking for an address (the house numbering system is extremely complex). If people want police help, they usually come to the *koban*. There are few police patrols except for traffic duty, and those that are undertaken are usually by bicycle. Police contact with communities is impressive — an officer visits every home twice a year, simply to determine who lives where.

Police in Japan have a very free hand. Instead of issuing a traffic ticket, an officer might have the motorist write a personal letter to the police chief, offering his apologies. Instead of effecting an arrest, an officer can have the disputants argue the case before him, and reach a conclusion that all parties can agree to. It is assumed that police have great latitude of discretion to dispose of a case, whereas in Canada the assumption (despite reality) is that the law is the law and the officer cannot use his discretion. In Japan the officer has a great deal of moral authority; in Canada the authority of the officer springs strictly from the law. In Japan enforcement is tailored specifically to the individual in question; in Canada the individual is categorized and dealt with no differently than anyone else who might have done the act complained of.

The objectives pursued in each country are quite different. In Japan the police are involved in a system that asks for a confession, for repentance, for appropriate signs of embarrassment. In Canada the system is combative — the accused bargains about the plea and is punished mostly in anger. Certainly the social situations in each country are markedly different, and Japanese crime levels are only a fraction of those in North America. But the comparison shows that different objectives can produce different results and different police attitudes.

Police goals and objectives have not been widely debated in Canada for a number of reasons, ranging from the timidity of the politician to the reluctance on the part of police organizations to enter a process that could reduce social status through job redefinition. But it is time that society was clearer about the objectives officers should be striving for as public servants. Setting down goals with clarity and precision would not only result in the public having more realistic expectations about performance, but would provide some yardstick for measuring police efficiency. Inevitably, some agreed-upon objectives will conflict due to the nature of the work, but it will be easier to make and judge choices when the objectives are set out in black and white.

The eight objectives outlined by Herman Goldstein in conjunction with the American Bar Association (cited in chapter 4) seem like a reasonable place to start, and bear repetition:

> 1. To prevent and control conduct widely recognized as threatening to life and property (serious crime).
> 2. To aid individuals who are in danger of physical harm, such as the victim of a criminal attack, or of an accident.
> 3. To protect constitutional guarantees, such as the right of free speech and assembly.
> 4. To facilitate the movement of people and vehicles.
> 5. To assist those who cannot care for themselves; the intoxicated, the addicted, the mentally ill, the physically disabled, the old, and the young.
> 6. To resolve conflict, whether it is between individuals, groups of individuals, or individuals and their government.
> 7. To identify problems that have the potential of becoming more serious problems for the individual citizen, for the police, or for the government.
> 8. To create and maintain a feeling of security in the community.[2]

These principles might not be exactly right for Canadian police forces (the note about ''constitutional guarantees'' rings strange, although the new Constitution has been in place for several years), but they do succinctly state the range of diverse activities that society wishes police to be involved in.

The debate could most easily begin by an approach to a local police commission, requesting that goals and objectives be adopted for the rest of the 1980s. The commission should be requested to have staff report on a particular set of objectives, such as Goldstein's, and then hear the response of interested members of the community. The openness of police organizations to improving community relations should help begin this process.

Clarifying objectives has a number of significant ramifications. It will help with decisions about police training, organizational structure, and the question of who should be encouraged to become police officers. And it will get the public into the basically uncharted sphere of police discretion. Discretion exists because there are different kinds of actions that can be taken depending on the goal to be reached. Once the goals are clear, then some kind of direction can be given with respect to discretion.

There are strong pressures against trying to structure discretion. Some claim that police have enough power already — why admit to the fact that they have more? Others argue that since police regularly exceed their authority now, setting down guidelines for the exercise of discretion won't be a useful fetter. Yet these arguments appear weak to those simply asking that police treatment be both fair and equal. Two individuals engaged in the same type of activity — such as quietly enjoying a glass of wine with a picnic in a public park — should be able to predict how they will be treated, rather than hoping that the officers will be sensible in each case.

To say that society could not tolerate a set of guidelines that actually instructs officers not to enforce certain laws at certain times is to misread how most people perceive social situations. There is a widespread feeling that police should intervene only when situations have spun out of control or are about to. The rest of the time, laws should only be enforced sparingly. Indeed, there are some who argue that laws exist only to be enforced in such situations, and that legislators never meant that they be enforced at all times. This is particularly true of laws relating to matters such as Sunday openings, parking, and social gambling. Discretion is expected in the enforcement of these kinds of laws. The officer is expected to look at a problem sensibly and perhaps decide that the enforcement of the law would not make sense. Officers do this now when they decide not to enforce laws about nudity and nude bathing on certain beaches, in the interests of respecting different social mores.

The best place to begin a discussion about structuring discretion is around present police practices. For instance, most police forces use an informal quota system for automobile offences. To gauge productivity, senior officers set goals for officers, indicating that a certain number of tickets for moving violations are expected to be issued on a monthly basis, as well as a certain number of parking tickets. But the police are not eager to admit the use of quotas. We should admit that such quotas (either formal or informal) do exist, debate whether the idea of quotas is a good one or not, and if so, what the quota might be.

A second example deals with speeding offences. It is widely recognized that officers usually dispense speeding tickets when the offender is exceeding posted limits by ten kilometres per hour. That is certainly an exercise of police discretion. It is probably widely supported by the public at large as being reasonable, but there should be some public discussion of this habit to ensure that it indeed is what society wants.

A third example is in the sticky area of morality and community standards. What should the police consider to be pornographic or offensive, when the whole area of law and morality is so unclear? Public discussion could help to resolve these problems and give police guidelines in which to operate. For instance, it could be decided that the police role was to negotiate with the suspected offender to limit activities to a less offensive or less public level — that might be the best way for the police to exercise their discretion in these situations. Or it could be decided that before any charges were laid for breaching community standards, police should give a warning so that the offending party can at least take steps to achieve behaviour that is more in keeping with perceived standards. In both kinds of responses, officers would be exercising their discretion after a public discussion, rather than after a decision is made only within the police organization.

K.C. Davis suggests that the first step to structuring discretion is a public admission that all laws are not enforced all the time, followed by a recognition that selective law enforcement is the norm. The above three examples exhibit both characteristics. It will then be necessary to have policing authorities agree to help formulate guidelines, much in the way they have been devised for specialized police services such as youth squads, as discussed in chapter 3. In all likelihood this will be a difficult step for police authorities, since like other bureaucracies they will be unhappy about the idea of losing unfettered control. But it will help to forge strong links between a community and its police, even if the discussion only takes place around several limited areas of police work.

Structuring discretion will not be easy, even though it follows directly from a definition of goals and objectives and a realization that some of those goals conflict, giving wide freedom of choice to the officer. But it is an important step, since only by structuring discretion in some reasonable manner can members of the public be assured that they will be treated fairly and equally by officers. It will also help provide the officer with the clearest advice about what the community expects of police and the choices they must make on a daily basis. Structuring discretion is doing nothing more than bringing into the open a decision-making process that for too long has been hidden away.

Raising questions about goals and objectives, and about the structuring of discretion, brings into focus the nature of police governing bodies. Regardless of their exact composition and whether there is a majority of provincial appointees on police commissions, it is hard to find a commission in Canada that is on the leading edge of debate over police matters. Most commissions are known best for their secrecy and the fact that only rarely does a full-fledged policy debate occur of the type that can be expected at a city council meeting.

This unsatisfactory situation must change. Police commissions must become the principal forum for debate, provoking the public to struggle with the difficult issues faced in policing, this most important of public institutions. A police commission should be setting the agenda for a public discussion of matters such as prostitution, crime prevention, public safety, and police practices. If the one body that deals with these issues on a daily basis won't begin discussion on these points, who will?

Two changes are required to make police commissions more effective. First, membership should be enlarged to nine or ten members. This will produce two positive results: more voices can be heard, ensuring a wider spectrum of opinion; and there will be large enough numbers to provide the critical mass necessary for debate. Too often the discussion of important matters is shallow because the individuals involved are worried that they will be centred out and mocked. A larger commission could provide the protection necessary for new opinions to emerge and be heard.

Second, commissions must be representative of the various divergent groups in the community being policed. For too long, minority groups have not found voices to represent their interests on police commissions. Because they have been frozen out of discussion on policing matters, they have had to turn to confrontation (usually on the streets) to be heard. As long as this lockout continues, there is little chance that police commissions will help with reform.

Changing the composition of police commissions is not easy. As noted in chapter 1, the provincial government grabbed control of police commissions in Upper Canada in 1858 and has never let go. In provinces where there is a history of provincial appointments being made on the recommendation of the local council — the situation in Vancouver until 1981 — provincial authorities are now moving to act on their own behalf.

Choosing and Training Officers

Among suggestions for reforming police, none is more popular than to improve officer training. Some wish to ensure that more university graduates are on the force. Others ask that training include sessions on human dynamics, minority rights, and sexuality. In truth, most Canadian police forces have responded favourably to these suggestions, but the results hoped for do not appear to be materializing.

But focusing on training misses the source of the problem, which is the way officers are recruited. As shown in chapter 3, a police officer must start right at the bottom. All applicants are processed exactly the same way, and those who pass screening are subject to a standard training course. No allowances are made for age differentials, technical skills, formal educational achievements, or life experience. A recruit is a recruit.

The limitations set on entry reflect the idea that police officers are all of one kind, doing basically the same job, with varying degrees of emphasis in certain areas. There is a presumption that an officer must be a generalist, not a specialist, requiring the common training program. It also means that there is a bias in the selection process towards a certain idea of the "ideal" officer, one who is young, big and not yet established in life. Applicants who do not fit these criteria have a difficult time emerging from selection procedures. Hopefuls who have different qualities, such as specific social skills, a facility with languages, or academic achievements, are not barred, but their special strengths are seen as secondary.

The result of these limitations is that policing can never be a second career. Someone who has been unhappy in a profession will not be considered an acceptable recruit, usually because of the age factor. Someone who has learned valuable skills in management, whether in government or the private sector, will not be able to meet selection standards, again usually for reasons of age, but quite possibly because of the stringent physical requirements. A woman who has raised a family will never be considered acceptable. A teacher with ten years' experience will have difficulty qualifying, as will an experienced shop steward, a clergyman — the list goes on and on. It is difficult to think of any other job that is so particular that entry requirements prohibit a rich mix of people from being fairly considered as possible contenders. The only diversity in police forces, and it is modest, comes from those trained as officers in some other country (which probably allowed entry only from the bottom) who then emigrated to Canada.

The first change that must be made to bring variety to recruit selection is to dispense with the generalist notion and recognize instead that policing is made up of a bundle of different functions, most of which require various skills in varying degrees. Perhaps the skills most required to perform vehicular and foot patrols are not high, but that might be simply because these functions have come to reflect the low skill levels of the people performing them.

There are other areas of policing where varying skills and life experiences would be most helpful — detective work, interacting with lawyers, undercover work, management systems, negotiation, crime prevention, dealing with social misfits, intelligence gathering, community relations and so forth.

The variety of police tasks requires that there be differing entry points for individuals with different skills and experiences. If management needs an Italian-speaking candidate to work on youth services, then recruitment practices can be structured accordingly. That should be true for all recruits. The police should hire specific people to fill specific jobs.

This approach will drastically improve the recruitment system. Instead of continuing with the flawed approach of casting a wide net in the hope of attracting minorities, police can define who they need to do what. Police forces could then begin to be a fair reflection of the communities they serve.

The most revolutionary change to police training would be to require that it be held on the campus of an existing university. Recruits would then see their training as part of an educational experience that others in society were also engaged in, albeit in other disciplines. Recruits would pick up those educational experiences said to be the most important at a university — debating in coffee shops, discovering new ideas, going to exotic lectures and cultural experiences, realizing the complexity and the grandeur of human life, as well as its limitations.

The cost for police authorities of this change would be high in terms of lost control. On a university campus it would be impossible to force recruits into a dormitory setting — most would like to live as other students do, at home with their families or in shared accommodations with peers. Mass routine drills might have to disappear along with the bunk beds.

If one were only to address present training on its own terms, certain reforms could still be suggested. A curriculum should include approaches to goals and objectives, the exercise of discretion, the opportunities of specialization and the danger of police corruption. In short, teaching should be directed to learning about what it means to be a police officer in modern society, including the pressures that the job entails. Even within the severe limitations of present teaching methods, an exploration of these subjects would be of great help to the new recruit.

Managing Police

Managers within the police force have all come up from the bottom. They entered the force at the bottom of the ladder and slowly worked their way up through the ranks. Thus, all police managers share three characteristics: they have been in policing for most of their adult lives; they have managed to adapt their ideas well enough to those of previous police managers to have gained promotions; and they are in older age brackets. Managers in other bureaucracies instead show a range of work experiences, ages and relationships with previous managers.

There is a further distinction. In private business, and more and more frequently in the civil service, individuals are hired to perform management functions divorced from policy. People are hired not because they know how to make refrigerators, or how to be accountants, or how to sell clothing: they are hired because they are good at motivating people, at getting the best from them and making them happy and productive employees. Nuts-and-bolts skills are seen to be almost irrelevant to many management jobs.

Not so in policing. The managers in a police force come only from within the police community — usually from the very force itself. They are police first, and managers second. This means that management of police forces is not nearly as innovative or effective as in other organizations. Police managers tend to be undereducated compared to other managers, and are probably less *au courant* with fresh techniques that keep a bureaucracy humming at an acceptable level.

A handful of civilian managers has been added to some forces, but this change does not directly address the problem, since civilians have little status in a police force and are considered outsiders. The important management issues continue to be addressed by the police officers who have become managers.

Until the two general principles of generalist officers and entry only at the bottom are loosened up, it will be difficult for better police management practices to make themselves evident. In the meantime, positive changes are still possible. If the idea of managers from outside a force cannot be wholly embraced, it would still be very helpful for a large force to obtain the services of a senior manager from the private sector for several years, even on a civilian basis. If a senior manager from some large company like IBM or Stelco were plunked down in the middle of a large police force, that individual would have a host of suggestions for improving personnel policies, management techniques, job allocations, and productivity. This person could probably make suggestions for improving morale and increasing job satisfaction — two worrisome problems for police forces. While many police managers would have some difficulty in coping with the kinds of changes the outsider might want to make, the support from the rank and file to reasonable changes would probably give him a great deal of leverage. Further, this kind of placement would help link policing to other functions in society, so that there would be a better understanding on both sides as to how the world actually worked. This kind of cross-fertilization, which happens frequently now between the public and private sectors as well as within each, should be encouraged in the police.

Hiring a manager is hiring a specialist, someone who understands the specific job required for the police force to work well. Managers are not the only specialists who should be hired. As earlier discussion showed, when officers are permitted to specialize, their goals become clearer, they begin to structure discretion and their relationships with other social agencies improve. Specialization within police forces should be encouraged, so that there could be special sections with special skills for solving certain kinds of problems — to this end, the above suggested reform to recruitment would be invaluable. Of course, there will continue to be the need for officers who can do a bit of everything, just as every other bureaucracy needs such people.

Good managers experiment. They try doing things different ways, making different responses to see how productivity can be improved and employees can be more satisfied. They study the work that is being done, they do surveys about effectiveness, and they generally spend time and energy reflecting on the kinds of jobs the organization is performing.

Few of these actions now occur within police forces. The amount spent by forces on research and development work is either non-existent or minimal. Many private organizations make sure they allocate 2 or 3 per cent of the operating budget to management issues so that research and development is adequately funded. This kind of funding, which pays for itself many times over (as other organizations would testify), should be encouraged immediately — along with the retention or hiring of managers who know how to spend this money well. Only with a good data base can more reasonable decisions be made about how members of the police force can be most effectively used, to the benefit of the community as well as to their own satisfaction.

Improved management will certainly touch on the forging of better relations with the social agencies that policing, of necessity, must deal with. This is a matter of some importance, since the hostility felt between many of these agencies and the police is ingrained and interferes with the performance of each. Again, these changes are dependent on a recognition of the need to specialize some police functions.

From the public's point of view, the most pressing policing problem is the treatment of complaints. New management responses must be found that recognize complaints as a form of feedback. Reviewing complaints must be made routine in the same way that complaints against other civil servants are handled. Certainly there are very great distinctions between police and other civil servants, given police powers. But police must become much more relaxed about how the public perceives the role they play, and that in itself will help to resolve the substantial criticisms about police errors.

One starting point would be for a number of different forces to experiment with different approaches to complaints and then compare their results. Again, this kind of approach can best be explored by appropriate first-class managers who can look at problems from a management, rather than simply from a police, point of view.

Future Pressures

As more and more of the places frequented by the public are privately controlled, more and more police functions are carried out by private corporations. The number of public police officers has not declined in Canada — indeed it has grown rapidly over the last two decades — but patrol functions that public officers used to do are now carried out by private individuals who are not accountable to any public body. At the same time, a private justice system is being built beside the traditional publicly controlled criminal justice system.

This will pose extremely difficult questions for society. Should people be allowed to contract into private justice systems and then suffer the consequences, or should there be substantial public control of such systems? Should private police officers — many of whom might be armed in exactly the same way as public officers, as has happened in the United States — be required to undertake training of some kind? Do our notions of ''private'' property have to be amended so that rights now only secured on public property apply to mass private property? Should public police officers be available for private hire on an even broader basis than at present? Should the public and private forces compete?

These questions could cause turmoil and confusion as answers are forged by the force of events. And it could happen that reforms will suddenly be obsolete. These questions are best answered within the public realm: privately run policing firms must be subject to public scrutiny and control. At the present time, security firms and their employees must be registered — but this is the end, rather than the beginning, of public involvement. The registration step could be used to obtain information about the activities of these companies, with a view to setting recruitment standards and suggesting guidelines for the exercise of private powers on mass private property. Using registration requirements to begin looking more intensely at private policing seems an easy and necessary first step.

While private policing grows, public policing is facing a serious financial problem. Since the end of the Second World War, money has not been a problem for police forces until recently. As the population of all Canadian cities expanded, the number of officers grew rapidly, almost exceeding the rate at which management could cope with new recruits. Funds were available to buy whatever equipment was thought necessary, to build stations in new communities and to rebuild old stations. It seemed that police requests for funds were rarely denied.

But since 1980 the situation has changed. In many cities, population has stabilized, and so has construction activity. Assessments are no longer growing like topsy, and tax rates are beginning to rise inexorably. Now taxpayers worry about municipal expenditures, and their elected representatives look for ways to hold the line on spending.

At the same time, provincial governments also find themselves constrained financially. The recession of the early 1980s meant that deficits became more frequent and larger. Provinces found too that the federal government was no longer willing to dispense money with such abandon. New cash sources such as lotteries were sought out. But the simplest way for most provinces to ease financial woes was to reduce the money transferred to municipalities.

Transfer payments account for 10 to 15 per cent of provincial expenditures. These payments have become more conditional (i.e., tied to specific projects and not available as general revenue), or more limited. General provincial grants based on the population of an urban centre, or on assessment, have become stagnant, not even keeping pace with inflation. Cities have had to fund rising salaries from a constant sum.

The pressures of stunted growth and stagnant transfers led municipalities to "cut out fat." Then began tentative service cuts, with seemingly least-necessary services, and services to the least powerful (the poor), being pruned first. To date, police services have been adversely affected only in cities that have faced dire problems, such as Calgary, where layoffs have occurred. But these problems can be expected to intensify, particularly since the costs of policing services occupy such a large portion — up to 30 per cent — of the municipal budget. Police management will be forced to make some tough choices about the kinds of services that should be delivered and what the best delivery mechanisms are. With appropriate managers, this poses a most interesting challenge, that of making do with less. As has been previously argued, there appear to be ample opportunities to reduce police expenditures, for instance in patrol, without adversely affecting the protection of the public.

But it is entirely possible that rather than management responding creatively to the financial strictures, the response will be tough and uncooperative. Police unions might decide to dig their heels in, whether through strikes or shows of force. Police unions might decide to become more active politically against politicians who support police cutbacks, a prospect that would be sure to throw fear into the hearts of some politicians. The coming financial crunch might very well produce a police backlash that polarizes cities and subjects the municipal political system to the full, as yet untested, powers of police unions.

Two Visions of the Future

These two different approaches to the financial problem — the bright vision of creating a more responsive policing service, even with more modest funding, and the dark vision of the police becoming a more dominant polarized force in society — define the parameters of what could happen in the future. The best advocate of the bright vision is John Alderson.[3]

Alderson has been a police officer for all of his adult life, most recently as police chief of a semi-urban community south-east of London, England. His view of the future is based on four assumptions:

- Traditionally, policing has been a matter of enforcing a consensus. Now there is no clear consensus but rather a number of different ideas about what should happen and what is acceptable.
- Given the amount of crime that seems to occur, it is unreasonable to argue that the key to crime control lies with the criminal justice system. That system is simply too puny and delicate to bear the weight of excessive crime.
- People in society want both freedom and security, but police can't deliver both at once. Security can only be purchased with some infringement on freedom.
- Increased crime is the price of an increasingly free and unfettered society.

These assumptions are not particularly arguable at least in terms of the information and analysis presented in this book. Alderson draws two conclusions and proposes a course of action. He concludes that policing a community in a liberated, permissive society cannot rely solely on force and the criminal process. Other mechanisms must be found. As well, considerable coordination — certainly more than is now evident — will be required to create more and better public peace. Government agencies and private organizations both inside and outside the criminal justice system will have to work much more closely.

Alderson proposes that police should be the agency helping different interests in society become better integrated to contain crime. His is a concept of community policing, where the function of police is to "activate the sense of civic responsibility" in citizens. Police would activate people to become interested in public issues surrounding crime and the community, and then take appropriate actions. In this proactive role, police penetration of the community would be complete enough to give forces a full understanding of society so as to help it carry out its best wishes.

The police would call community meetings to discuss crime and order. They would help the community express ideas and concerns, and then help arrive at solutions. In essence, the police become community organizers.

Alderson used this approach with success in his own force, and elements of it are seen in other forces. In Detroit, mini-stations have been successfully established, and officers working from them play a strong role in organizing residents to improve neighbourhood safety through streetlighting, peepholes in doors, improved apartment house entrances and so on. Efforts at crime prevention have been far-reaching, with a great deal of initiative coming from police, and there has been a substantial drop in the incidence of crime, as well as improved feelings of neighbourliness. The Alderson approach is also seen in recent attempts to establish Neighbourhood Watch programs in many Canadian cities. Police help create a community group, lead in the discussion about crime prevention steps, and help erect Neighbourhood Watch signs. In Toronto there has been a further attempt to have police play a proactive role by stopping and chatting with people on the street, but there have been suggestions that this kind of action will be an intrusion on the rights of those whom police see as undesirables. One suspects that it is easy to give lip service to the kinds of ideas Alderson is advancing.

If there is a flaw in Alderson's vision, it has to do with the way people perceive policing. It is too much to ask that the public tolerate in its midst a person who knows a lot, has a handle on the power structure, and is there to help — but works for someone else. Most communities fear do-gooders, for the good reason that they have no control over them. The idea of a group policing itself, using paid community organizers, makes considerable sense if it can be worked out. But if that person works for some other body, distrust and suspicion are sure to set in. No community will be willing to put up with that kind of penetration.

Using police as a resource vis-à-vis crime seems reasonable. Having police do preventative work by working with neighbourhood groups seems acceptable. But the minute police begin to work both sides of the street — that is, pretending to act for one group while really acting for another, with a double agenda — the public will react negatively. Organizing a neighbourhood is about as far as a police officer (or for that matter anyone else) can go without creating overriding and negative suspicion.

The polar opposite to the view that police can become the servant of society, perhaps even the glue that binds it into a working whole, is the idea of police as authority figures that protect society from stumbling into error. The dark vision is that police will become a law unto themselves, that there will be no distinction between those who make the laws and those who enforce them. It is the vision of the totalitarian state.

Charles Reith defines two approaches to policing.[4] One is a democratic system where the ruling authority confers on members of the community as a whole the responsibility for securing and maintaining the observance of law. This arrangement ensures that those who make the laws do not enforce them. The other model has the ruling authority appointing its own agents to enforce the law, and is used by most despotic regimes. It is a style much in evidence in the latter part of the twentieth century in South America and Africa, and according to most writers, in the Soviet Union and many of its satellites.

The dark vision says ordinary people can't win against the police. The options are to obey them, to join them, or to foment revolution to overthrow police and the power structure they represent. It is a vision that is referred to occasionally in North America, particularly by minorities or political extremists, and some helpful analytical literature has been produced embodying this viewpoint.

This view is one not widely shared in Canadian cities. Most people want to believe in the police as an institution that promotes good, even if the bright vision of Alderson overstates the kind of support that police can have. The police are not perfectable, nor are they satanic. Police forces are organizations that should be reformed because they are without adequate direction and control. This is the reform vision, the vision that police can be made to respond more appropriately to the demands of society.

Where is change most likely to take place? Many urge that it occur where the problems seem most evident — in areas of police violence, where there is usually much publicity, and sometimes even the appointment of a royal commission to look into allegations. Yet in all these cases, it seems that the inquiry is into the facts of the specific case and not into the kinds of changes that must be made to improve police behaviour. Perhaps reform is not best provoked through assaults on police violence.

Others start with police deviance as a whole, and ask for changes here. Some ask for a change in educational content, increased educational standards, or higher selection standards, to produce better officers.

In short, there are many approaches to reforming police. Success depends on exactly where the pressures are applied. Those who have sought reform by attacking police violence and other forms of deviance are too easily rebutted with the claim that there are bad apples in every barrel. As this book has tried to point out, many of the changes required are structural in nature. The problems are deep-rooted and require a fresh look at what police do, what we expect of them, and the tools that we give them. Often the result of faulty expectations is disillusionment, rather than critical analysis. We need to look long and hard at policing problems and formulate a plan to ensure that police are in tune with current social values and that they reach a level of productivity our society expects.

As has been mentioned, the hostile reaction that greets even the most constructive criticism of the police has stifled discussion in the past. A continuation of this knee-jerk reaction will only perpetuate the present vacuum surrounding the organization and methodology of policing. As long as policing issues are decided solely by a handful of career officers and malleable politicians, little of substance will change. The reform of urban policing — now long overdue — will be of immense benefit to both the public and the rank-and-file police officer.

Notes

Chapter 1

1   See Philip C. Stenning, "The Role of Police Boards and Commissions as Institutions of Municipal Police Governance," in *Organizational Police Deviance*, ed. Clifford D. Shearing (Toronto: Butterworths, 1981), p. 161.

2   For the only substantial history of policing in Ontario and the formation of the Ontario Provincial Police, see Dahn H. Higley, *OPP: The History of the Ontario Provincial Police* (Toronto: Queen's Printer, 1984).

3   Lorne Brown and Caroline Brown, *An Unauthorized History of the RCMP* (Toronto: James Lorimer, 1978), p. 10. This book is a helpful antidote to the fawning literature on the RCMP.

4   See Irving Abella, ed., *On Strike, Six Key Labour Struggles in Canada, 1919-49* (Toronto: James Lorimer, 1979). A brief history of the Winnipeg General Strike is given in chapter 1. In the five other strikes recounted here, local police sided with strikers in all but one instance.

5   See A.K. McDougall, "Policing in Ontario" (Ph.D. thesis, University of Western Ontario, 1971).

6   Solicitor General of Canada, *Selected Trends in Canadian Criminal Justice* (Ottawa, October, 1981).

Chapter 2

1   See Solicitor General of Canada, *Selected Trends in Canadian Criminal Justice* (Ottawa, October, 1981). This booklet provides much of the information in the next few pages.

2   Ontario, Provincial Secretariat for Justice, *Crime in Ontario 1980* (Toronto: Government of Ontario, 1982).

3   Ibid.

4   See Ontario, Provincial Secretariat for Justice, *Justice Statistics Ontario 1980* (Toronto, 1980), pp. 22-23.

5   Leon Radzinowicz and Joan King, *The Growth of Crime* (Harmondsworth, Middlesex: Pelican Books, 1979), p. 28.

6   Ibid., chap. 1.

7   Ibid., p. 301.

8   Richard V. Ericson, *Reproducing Order* (Toronto: University of Toronto Press, 1982), p. 159.

9   See James Q. Wilson, "Thinking about Crime," *Atlantic Monthly*, September, 1983, p. 88.

10 Solicitor General, *Selected Trends*, p. 17.

11 Heather Robertson, *Reservations Are for Indians* (Toronto: James Lorimer, 1970), pp. 243-44.

12 Jerome H. Skolnick, a California criminologist, argues that for all reasonable purposes the police are the justice system, acting as accuser, judge and punisher. See Skolnick, *Justice Without Trial* (Toronto: John Wiley and Sons, 1976).

13 Radzinowicz and King, *Growth of Crime*, chap. 3.

14 See Herbert Packer, *The Limits of the Criminal Sanction* (Englewood Cliffs, N.J.: Prentice-Hall, 1967).

15 P.B. Weston and K.M. Wells, *The Administration of Justice* (Englewood Cliffs, N.J.: Prentice-Hall, 1967).

16 See chapter 3 for a discussion of the Kansas City study.

17 Wilson, "Thinking about Crime," pp. 86-87; see note 9 above.

18 The term is from Radzinowicz, *Growth of Crime*, chap. 2.

[19] See ibid.

[20] Solicitor General, *Selected Trends*, p. 10.

[21] Ericson, *Reproducing Order*, p. 203.

[22] These definitions come from D.R. Cressey's brilliant booklet *Organized Crime and Criminal Organization* (Cambridge, Mass.: W. Heffer & Sons, 1971).

[23] William Kelly and Norah Kelly, *Policing in Canada* (Toronto: Macmillan, 1976), p. 467.

[24] See ibid., pp. 455-56. The authors also discuss the Lucien Rivard case and other examples of organized crime and the criminal justice system.

Chapter 3

[1] While the RCMP, the OPP and the QPP play some role in municipal policing, it is limited. More than two-thirds of police personnel work for municipal forces. See Solicitor General of Canada, *Selected Trends in Canadian Criminal Justice* (Ottawa, October, 1981).

[2] See William G. Gay et al, *Improving Patrol Productivity*, vol. 1, *Routine Patrol* (Washington, D.C.: National Institute of Law Enforcement and Criminal Justice, Law Enforcement Assistance Administration, U.S. Department of Justice, July, 1977), p. 3.

[3] Ibid., p. 9.

[4] Ibid., pp. 62-63.

[5] Ibid., p. 65.

[6] Richard V. Ericson, *Reproducing Order* (Toronto: University of Toronto Press, 1982), pp. 88-89.

[7] Ibid., p. 91.

[8] O.W. Wilson, *Police Administration*, 4th ed. (New York: McGraw-Hill, 1977).

[9] Ericson, *Reproducing Order*, p. 86. Charges followed in less than 5 per cent of such stops.

[10] Ibid., pp. 78-79.

[11] Ibid., p. 54.

[12] Ibid. See chapter 3. The study involved 348 shifts during 1978.

[13] Ibid., pp. 175-76.

[14] Ibid., p. 206.

[15] Herman Goldstein, *Policing a Free Society* (Cambridge, Mass.: Ballinger Publishing, 1977), p. 52.

[16] Richard V. Ericson, *Making Crime* (Toronto: Butterworths, 1981), chap. 2.

[17] Ibid., p. 215.

[18] Ibid., p. 43.

[19] Ibid., p. 136. For a fuller discussion of the role of informers, see pages 127f and Jerome Skolnick, *Justice Without Trial* (Toronto: John Wiley and Sons, 1976), chap. 6.

[20] Ibid., p. 159.

[21] Ibid., p. 165.

[22] Ibid., p. 170.

[23] Ibid., pp. 187-88.

[24] Ibid., p. 199.

[25] All information regarding the Youth Liaison Service is taken from Golden Leeson and Arn Snyder, ''Specialized Police Response to the Juvenile: The Ottawa Youth Liaison Section,'' in *The Police Function in Canada*, ed. W.T. McGrath and M.P. Mitchell (Toronto: Methuen, 1981), pp. 197-210. The authors are both officers in the Ottawa force.

[26] Ibid., p. 198.

[27] Ibid., p. 203.

[28] Ibid., pp. 204-5.

[29] For a further discussion of the Metro Toronto Domestic Response Team, see the ''Interim Evaluation'' prepared by the Sutcliffe Group, presented to Metro Toronto Council, November 3, 1981.

[30] See McDonald Commission of Inquiry Concerning Certain Activities of the RCMP, *Second Report*, vol. 1, pp. 508-9.

[31] John T. Clement, ''Review into the Standards and Recruitment Practises of the Metro Toronto Police Force''

(Submitted to the Metro Board of Commissioners of Police, March, 1980).

[32] Hickling/Johnston, Management Consultants, "Weighted Selection Standards System" (Study for the Metro Toronto Police Commission, September, 1980), p. 20.

[33] Ibid., p. 22.

[34] Ibid.

[35] Ibid., Appendix E.

[36] Ibid., Appendix F.

[37] "Report of the Task Force on the Racial and Ethnic Implications of Police Hiring, Training, Promotion and Career Development," July, 1980 (Submitted to the Solicitor General of Ontario). See pages 55-56.

[38] Arnold Bruner, "Report to City Council on the Bathhouse Raids" (Toronto, 1981), p. 86.

[39] Alan Grant, *The Police: A Policy Paper* (Ottawa: Law Reform Commission of Canada, 1980), pp. 65-66.

[40] Goldstein, *Policing a Free Society*, pp. 288-91.

[41] Ibid., p. 259.

[42] The Vancouver police force lists four areas of recruit training: investigation and patrol; legal studies; traffic studies; and social sciences.

[43] My thanks to Clive Paul, Staff Sergeant, Training and Development Section, Hamilton-Wentworth Regional Police, for this information.

[44] Brian A. Grosman, *Police Command* (Toronto: Macmillan, 1975), pp. 13-14.

[45] Ibid.

[46] See "In the Matter of an Appeal to the Ontario Police Commission by Constable Edward Murphy," decision dated December 12, 1983.

[47] Police strikes have been infrequent in Canada, although they have happened in the late 1970s and early 1980s in Eastern Canada as legislation became more permissive. Evidently Metro Toronto Police were ten minutes away from a wildcat strike in 1980 over wage parity with Toronto firemen, but they were talked out of it by Chief Harold Adamson.

[48] For a description of the strike and its effect on Montreal, see Brian McKenna and Susan Purcell, *Drapeau* (Toronto: Clarke Irwin, 1980), pp. 206-17.

[49] The two-man cruiser was invoked by police personnel as a safety measure. In fact, a 1976 study by Robin D. Hale for the Waterloo Regional Police, "Two Man Police Cars: Logic vs Emotion," argues that not only are two-man cars 30 per cent less efficient than one-man cars, but on the basis of reliable evidence, two-man cars are much more dangerous for officers. The study notes that two-man cars probably provoke carelessness in dangerous situations and that the delay forced by a one-man car seeking extra help is a margin of safety for the officers involved.

[50] Dennis Forcese of the Department of Sociology and Anthropology, Carleton University, has written most convincingly about these matters. See particularly "Police Unionism: Employee Management Relations in Canadian Police Forces," *Canadian Police College Journal*, vol. 4, no. 2 (1980).

[51] See C.D. Shearing and P.C. Stenning, *Private Security and Private Justice* (Toronto: Institute for Research on Public Policy, 1982), p. 4; and Clifford Shearing, Margaret Farnell and Philip Stenning, *Contract Security in Ontario* (Toronto: Centre of Criminology, University of Toronto, 1980), chap. 4.

[52] See Shearing, Farnell and Stenning, *Contract Security*, chap. 6.

[53] Ibid., pp. 238-40.

[54] Ibid.

Chapter 4

[1] Estimate of Toronto Police Chief Jack Aykroyd, 1980.

[2] For the American view — that liberty comes first — as applied to the Canadian context, see Edgar Z. Friedenberg, *Deference to Authority* (White Plains, N.Y.: M.E.

Sharpe, 1980). For examples of police wrongdoing condoned in the service of order, see Jeff Sallot, *Nobody Said No* (Toronto: James Lorimer, 1979).

3 The best exposition of this approach is Centre for Research on Criminal Justice, *The Iron Fist and the Velvet Glove* (Berkeley, Calif., 1977).

4 See "Second Annual Report of the Office of Public Complaints Commissioner, 1983" (Toronto), p. 30.

5 Clifford D. Shearing, ed., *Organizational Police Deviance* (Toronto: Butterworths, 1981), p. 9.

6 For a further elaboration of this theory, see Jerome H. Skolnick, *Justice Without Trial* (Toronto: John Wiley and Sons, 1976).

7 Herman Goldstein, *Policing a Free Society* (Cambridge, Mass.: Ballinger Publishing, 1977), p. 35.

8 Solicitor General of Canada, "Report on the Proceedings, Workshop on Police Productivity and Performance" (May, 1978), p. 45. The author cited is Jerome A. Needle.

9 Ibid., p. 58.

10 Ontario Police Commission, "Information and Police Management in Ontario" (February, 1981), p. 22. The eight forces studied were London, Durham Region, Ottawa, Peterborough, Toronto, Halton Region, Hamilton-Wentworth, and York Region.

11 This is not, however, a matter on which there is widespread agreement. See Solicitor General, "Workshop," p. 78.

12 Ibid., p. 126. The two-year study collected information from 153 American jurisdictions.

13 Ibid., p. 84.

14 Ibid., p. 145.

15 Alan Grant, *The Police: A Policy Paper* (Ottawa: Law Reform Commission of Canada, 1980), pp. 181-82.

16 Goldstein, *Policing a Free Society*, p. 28.

17 William Kelly and Norah Kelly, *Policing in Canada* (Toronto: Macmillan, 1976), p. 201.

18 McDonald Commission, *Second Report*, vol. 2, p. 904.

[19] K.C. Davis, *Discretionary Justice* (Baton Rouge: Louisiana State University, 1969). A short and brilliant book.

[20] For precise language regarding these powers, see the Criminal Code of Canada.

[21] See note 1, chap. 1.

[22] See K.C. Palmer, "Police Governance in Waterloo Region" (Background study for the Waterloo Review Commission, 1979).

[23] See Philip C. Stenning, "The Role of Police Boards and Commissions as Institutions of Municipal Police Governance," in *Organizational Police Deviance*, ed. Clifford D. Shearing (Toronto: Butterworths, 1981), p. 197.

[24] Ibid., pp. 194-95.

Chapter 5

[1] The following books have been helpful in this analysis: William H. Kroes and Joseph J. Hurell, Jr., eds., *Job Stress and the Police Officer* (Bethseda, Md.: U.S. Department of Health, 1975); Michael Banton, *The Policeman in the Community* (London: Tavistock Publications, 1964); William A. Westley, *Violence and the Police* (Cambridge, Mass.: MIT Press, 1970); and A. Neiderhoffer, *Behind the Shield* (Garden City, N.Y.: Doubleday, 1967). Also see Jerome H. Skolnick, *Justice Without Trial* (Toronto: John Wiley and Sons, 1976), chap. 2.

[2] For hard evidence of discrimination of minorities in day-to-day police work, see Richard V. Ericson, *Reproducing Order* (Toronto: University of Toronto Press, 1982).

[3] Clifford D. Shearing, ed., *Organizational Police Deviance* (Toronto: Butterworths, 1981), p. 4.

[4] Ibid., p. 9.

[5] Ibid., citing Martin Friedland's *Detention Before Trial*.

[6] Ibid., p. 26.

[7] See decision of the Police Complaints Board, August 24, 1984, re complainant David Edward Footman.

8   Herman Goldstein, *Policing a Free Society* (Cambridge, Mass.: Ballinger Publishing, 1977), pp. 194-95.
9   See Regulation set out in chapter 2, above.
10 See "Second Annual Report of the Office of the Public Complaints Commissioner, 1983."
11 Jeff Sallot, *Nobody Said No* (Toronto: James Lorimer, 1979), pp. 36-37. This book gives a good picture of the dirty tricks mentioned here. For a fuller discussion, see the three-volume report of the McDonald Commission.
12 Ibid., p. 38.
13 Ibid., p. 194.

Chapter 6

1   See David H. Bayley, *Forces of Order* (Berkeley, Calif.: University of California Press, 1976), for a much fuller description.
2   Herman Goldstein, *Policing a Free Society* (Cambridge, Mass.: Ballinger Publishing, 1977), p. 35.
3   John Alderson's most interesting book is *Policing Freedom* (Plymouth: MacDonald & Evans, 1979).
4   Charles Reith, *The Blind Eye of History* (Montclair, N.J.: Patterson Smith, 1975).

Further Reading

As mentioned in the introduction, there are great gaps in police literature. Little material apart from that done by Ericson actually describes day-to-day police work, leaving a void when it comes to real-life experience. The history of Canadian policing is still to be written, and apart from Higley's book, there is little that is helpful in describing the past. The books below are the most useful that I was able to discover, although my fear was that having found so little, I must have missed a great deal. What my continued search revealed was just more of the same pulp describing heroic deeds, and personal accounts of police experience.

Centre for Research and Criminal Justice. *The Iron Fist and the Velvet Glove*. Berkeley, Calif., 1977. A description of police as hostile agents of an evil state, with particular reference to the United States.

Cressey, D.R. *Organized Crime and Criminal Organization*. A short but brilliant discussion of organized crime and how it works.

Davis, K.C. *Discretionary Justice*. A short and enlightening discussion on the subject of discretion and how it should be structured.

Ericson, Richard V. *Reproducing Order: A Study of Police Patrol Work*. Toronto: University of Toronto Press, 1982. A case study of patrol work in the Region of Peel, just to the west of Toronto; this is one of the few books where one can find hard data about what police actually do on patrol. The survey was completed in the mid-1970s over some hundreds of shifts, with the cooperation of the Peel police.

Ericson, Richard V. *Making Crime: A Study of Detective Work*. Toronto: Butterworths, 1981. The parallel book to *Reproducing Order*, but this time on Peel detectives.

Goldstein, Herman. *Policing a Free Society*. Cambridge, Mass.: Ballinger Publishing, 1977. The best general study of police issues in the United States, generally applicable to Canada.

Grant, Alan. *The Police: A Policy Paper*. Ottawa: Law Reform Commission of Canada, 1980. A stimulating discussion of organizational and recruitment issues in Canada.

Grosman, Brian A. *Police Command: Decisions and Discretion*. Toronto: Macmillan, 1975. This book discusses questions of police leadership with some references to Canada.

Higley, Dahn D. *O.P.P. The History of the Ontario Provincial Police Force*. Toronto: The Queen's Printer, 1984. The only helpful book giving the history of one Canadian police force.

Kelly, William, and Kelly, Nora. *Policing in Canada*. Toronto: Macmillan, 1976. A general survey of policing in Canada that seems to avoid all the difficult questions.

McGrath, W.T., and Mitchell, M.P., eds. *The Police Function in Canada*. Toronto: Methuen, 1981. A collection of seventeen short essays by different authors — making a quite uneven book — meant as a primary criminal justice course reader.

Ontario, Provincial Secretariat for Justice. *Crime in Ontario*. Toronto: Government of Ontario, 1982. A thirty-four page booklet of charts and facts relating to Ontario.

Ontario, Provincial Secretariat for Justice. *Justice Statistics Ontario 1980*. Toronto, 1980. Very detailed statistics for Ontario in 172 pages.

Radzinowicz, Leon, and King, Joan. *The Growth of Crime*. 1977; Harmondsworth, Middlesex: Pelican Books, 1979. A most readable survey of crime and related issues in the Western world.

Shearing, Clifford D., ed. *Organizational Police Deviance*. Toronto: Butterworths, 1981. Seven essays on policing in Canada, by different authors but all on the subject of police deviance with the exception of Philip C. Stenning's article on the history of police boards. The examples of deviance are most thought-provoking.

Skolnick, Jerome H. *Justice Without Trial*. Toronto: John Wiley and Sons, 1976 (now in paperback). An excellent, thought-provoking study of police in society, with examples from California.

Solicitor General of Canada. *Selected Trends in Canadian Criminal Justice*. Ottawa, October, 1981. Available from Programs Branch, Ministry of the Solicitor General. A summary of charts and issues in thirty-six helpful pages.

Solicitor General of Canada. *Workshop on Police Productivity and Performance*. Ottawa, 1978. While it suffers from being a recounting of a two-day conference, it is quite useful in elucidating questions of productivity.

Other Books in the Canadian Issues Series

The West
The History of a Region in Confederation
J.F. CONWAY

Since settlers first tried to eke out a living on the banks of the Red River, Western Canadians have felt that the West's place in the Canadian scheme of things is a subordinate one. John Conway's book is a history of Confederation from the point of view of the four western provinces. Conway shows that although the focus of western dissatisfaction may have changed in recent years, the root cause of having to "buy dear and sell cheap" remains.

"A must for anyone who wishes to know about the recent economic and political past of Western Canada." — Lethbridge *Herald*.

"A provocative study of the historical roots of Western alienation." — Regina *Leader-Post*.

Ethics and Economics
Canada's Catholic Bishops on the Economic Crisis
GREGORY BAUM and DUNCAN CAMERON

The most talked-about political manifesto of recent years is "Ethical Reflections on the Economic Crisis," issued in early 1983 by Canada's Catholic bishops. The statement's impact reverberated through political, church and business circles, because of its trenchant critique of the structural problems of Canadian society and the economy.

This book takes the issues raised by the bishops several steps further. ''Ethical Reflections'' is included, followed by two wide-ranging commentaries: one from an ethical point of view, by Gregory Baum; the other from an economic perspective, by Duncan Cameron. Several earlier statements by the bishops are also included as a guide to further reading on this subject.

''A major contribution to the understanding of the Canadian Church.'' — *Catholic New Times*.

''The bishops' proposals are given fresh force by Baum and Cameron.'' — *Globe and Mail*.

Oil and Gas
Ottawa, the Provinces and the Petroleum Industry
JAMES LAXER

For more than a decade, the oil industry and energy policy have been a central issue in Canadian economic and political life. *Oil and Gas* offers an overview of these turbulent years and fresh insight into the motives of the main players: Ottawa, Alberta and other producing provinces, the oil majors such as Imperial, the Canadian companies like Petro-Canada, the OPEC cartel and the U.S. government.

''Provocative reading'' — *Canadian Public Policy*.

Women and Work
Inequality in the Labour Market
PAUL PHILLIPS and ERIN PHILLIPS

Why are women still second-class citizens at work? To answer this question, Paul and Erin Phillips trace women's involvement in the paid labour market, and in labour unions, throughout Canadian history. They document the disadvantages that women face today and examine the explanations that have been forwarded for the persistence of these problems. Chapters are devoted to the effect of technological changes such as the microelectronic ''chip'' on women's work and to proposals for bringing about equality in the labour market.

''A fine salute to the strong body of materials on women's work that has sprung into being in the last decade.'' — *Toronto Star*.

Regional Disparities
New Updated Edition
PAUL PHILLIPS

This is the first and only book to address the perennial problem of the gap between ''have'' and ''have-not'' provinces. In this new updated edition of this popular study, Paul Phillips examines developments such as the National Energy Program, the Alberta-Ottawa oil deal, the industrial slump in Central Canada, and the increased prospects for economic growth in resource-rich provinces.

''A concise, convincing overview.'' — *Quill & Quire*.

The New Canadian Constitution
DAVID MILNE

The New Canadian Constitution explains just what everyone wanted out of the constitution-making process, who got what, and what the final results mean for Canadians. Of special interest is the concluding chapter, which examines the nature of the new constitution in terms of both interests, issues and accidents that shaped it, and its own strengths and weaknesses.

"...a straightforward and comprehensive narrative." — *Globe and Mail*.

Industry in Decline
RICHARD STARKS

Summing up proposals from labour, the NDP, the business community and the Science Council of Canada, Richard Starks, a financial journalist formerly with the *Financial Post*, examines the growing consensus that Canada needs a new industrial strategy.

"The beauty of the book and its importance is its straightforward, uncomplicated, journalistic style, and its price." — *Canadian Materials*.

Rising Prices
H. LUKIN ROBINSON

This book explains why prices are so high today and tells us what inflation is all about. The author defines mystifying terms like "cost-push" inflation and applies them to everyday situations.

"A masterpiece of popular economics. The book swiftly moves from the very elementary to the very complex...without losing its readers along the way." — *Canadian Forum*.

Out of Work
CY GONICK

Cy Gonick shows why the Canadian economy is failing to create jobs for all the people who want to work, and why government is unwilling to take the necessary steps to deal with the issue.

"Gonick is one of the few political scientists around who can put complicated arguments into readable English. He talks more sense in less space than any other contemporary commentator." — *Books in Canada*.

Also of Interest from James Lorimer & Company

Up Against City Hall

JOHN SEWELL

John Sewell is probably the best-known reformer in Canadian municipal politics. This is Sewell's own account of his passage from community organizing to Toronto City Hall.

An Unauthorized History of the RCMP

LORNE BROWN and CAROLINE BROWN

This muckraking classic shows how the celebrated "dirty tricks" carried out by the RCMP in Quebec simply continued a long-standing tradition of political campaigns by the Mounties.

Nobody Said No
The Real Story About How the Mounties Always Get Their Man

JEFF SALLOT

Based on the proceedings of the McDonald Commission into RCMP wrongdoing, *Nobody Said No* details the habitual lawbreaking of the RCMP in its campaign against the nationalist left in Quebec after 1970.

Rumours of War

RON HAGGART and AUBREY E. GOLDEN

This classic study of the 1970 October Crisis focuses on the logic of the widespread arrests of political activists, their internments and interrogations.

The Life and Death of Anna Mae Aquash

JOHANNA BRAND

An investigation into the unsolved murder of Anna Mae Aquash, a Canadian active in the Native rights movement. Johanna Brand tells the alarming story of a secret war between the FBI, the RCMP and the American Indian Movement.

Sweethearts
The Builders, the Mob and the Men

CATHERINE WISMER

In this study of organized crime involvement in legitimate business, Catherine Wismer zeroes in on the mobsters, extortionists, hit men and builders who moved in on Toronto's thriving highrise apartment business during the 1960s.

How to Fight for What's Right
The Citizen's Guide to Public Interest Law

JOHN SWAIGEN

Written for citizens who are fighting back in court against abuses by government and big business, this guidebook has been widely acclaimed by environmentalists, civil rights organizations, consumer groups and community law clinics.